Rarely does a book live up to its own billing, but this one exceeds it! The book is an inspiring and practical combination of touching stories and wonderful rituals; weaving together appropriate Scriptures, challenging reflection questions and processes, and prayer. What a wonderful revelation of the sacredness of parenting. We hope every parish will find a way to put this treasure in the hands of every baptismal and first Communion family. It's that rich!

> —**Kathleen and James McGinnis**, international co-coordinators of the Parenting for Peace and Justice Network

More Than Meets the Eye is itself more—and better—than I could have ever imagined! It appeals on many levels: the family stories, the method of interpreting them, the rituals for praying and celebrating their meaning. Every family member can discover in this book a fresh, exciting, and deeper path into a fundamental truth: God loves us enough to become one of us and remains there in daily events and relationships—if we can only see beyond what meets the eye.

> —**Richard McCord**, U.S. Catholic Bishops, Secretariat for Family, Laity, Women, and Youth

What a refreshing treasury of real stories from real families, stories that engender memories, smiles, and tears in the reader. An ideal resource for family workshops, retreats, and gatherings of all kinds. Sure to fire up discussion on how the daily minutiae of life in the kitchen equals the sacramentality of life in the pew.

> —**Dolores Curran**, author of *Dolores Curran on Family Prayer*

More
Than
Meets
the
Eye

More Than Meets the Eye

Finding God in the Creases and Folds of Family Life

Mary Jo Pedersen   Thomas Greisen   Ronald Wasikowski

Saint Mary's Press
Christian Brothers Publications
Winona, Minnesota

To our families and friends, who have inspired us to notice, name, and reverence the sacred in family living.

We are grateful to those family members who willingly shared the raw experiences within their families as stories for this book. We thank them for the privilege of entering their stories and sharing them with others.

We are also grateful to the family who extended gracious hospitality to us in the mountains of Colorado. The peaceful space permitted us to practice our own depth perception.

Genuine recycled paper with 10% post-consumer waste.
Printed with soy-based ink.

The publishing team included Leif Kehrwald and Robert P. Stamschror, development editors; Laurie A. Berg, copy editor; Brooke E. Saron, production editor; Hollace Storkel, typesetter; Cären Yang, designer; cover photo, PhotoDisc, Inc.; produced by the graphics division of Saint Mary's Press.

The acknowledgments continue on page 151.

Printed in the United States of America

Printing: 9 8 7 6 5 4 3 2 1

Year: 2008 07 06 05 04 03 02 01 00

ISBN 0-88489-594-7

Library of Congress Cataloging-in-Publication Data

Greisen, Thomas.
    More than meets the eye : finding God in the creases and folds of family life / Thomas Greisen, Mary Jo Pedersen, Ronald Wasikowski.
    p. cm.
    ISBN 0-88489-594-7 (pbk. : alk. paper)
    1. Family—Religious life. 2. Family—Religious aspects—Catholic Church. I. Pedersen, Mary Jo. II. Wasikowski, Ronald. III. Title.
    BX2351 .G74 2000
    249—dc21
                                                          00-009382

Contents

Prologue

The real voyage of discovery consists not in seeking new land-scapes, but in having new eyes.

(Marcel Proust)

Have you ever spent a good length of time with a patch over your eye, seeing life with just one eye open? If you have, you know that depth perception is lost. Everything seems flat rather than three-dimensional. This is because each eye sees a slightly different angle of the same object. And when these two "visions" are put together, we can tell distances and the texture of things. Seeing with both eyes adds depth!

The same is true when we talk about our "vision" of God. Depth perception of God means we notice the Divine at work in a variety of ways. Let's look at the following story from the Scrip-tures:

[Elijah] got up, and ate and drank; then he went in the strength of that food forty days and forty nights to Horeb the mount of God. At that place he came to a cave, and spent the night there.

Then the word of the LORD came to him, saying . . . "Go out and stand on the mountain before the LORD, for the LORD is to pass by." Now there was a great wind, so strong that it was splitting mountains and breaking rocks in pieces before the LORD, but the LORD was not in the wind; and after the wind an earthquake, but the LORD was not in the earthquake; and after the earthquake a fire, but the LORD was not in the fire; and after the fire a sound of sheer silence. When Elijah heard it, he wrapped his face in his mantle and went out and stood at the entrance of the cave. Then there came a voice to him.

(1 Kings 19:8–13)

The early Israelites expected the presence of God to be found in heavy winds, an earthquake, or a fire. These were the traditional ways of theophany (manifestations of God), even from the time of Moses. In his encounter with God, what Elijah learns, and teaches us, is that God is found not only in the fire, wind, and earthquake, but this time in "a sound of sheer silence." Depending upon the particular translation, this paradoxical Hebrew phrase is also translated as "the sound of a gentle breeze" (The Jerusalem Bible), "a tiny whispering sound" (New American Bible), or "a still small voice" (Revised Standard Version). All these versions attempt to capture God's mysterious yet real presence. Spiritually speaking, this biblical story expands our understanding that God is found not merely in the noisy, profound, earth-shaking moments but also in the tiny whisperings of life.

"Seeing" God in the small, quiet parts of life involves more than eyesight. Religious depth perception necessitates seeing with our whole self, as Saint Ambrose (c. 339–397) comments:

> Do not then believe only what the eyes of your body tell you. What is not seen is here more truly seen, for what is seen belongs to time but what is not seen belongs to eternity. What is not comprehended by the eyes but is seen by the mind and the soul is seen in a truer and deeper sense.

("On the Mysteries," pp. 491–492)

What do Elijah and Ambrose have to say to families? Generally speaking, like Elijah, families expect to find God in the conventional ways: praying together, liturgies and celebrations at church, religion classes, and the like (the "fire, wind, and earthquake" events of families' religious practice). Just as God stretched Elijah's experience of the Divine, present in the whisper, the challenge to families is to encounter God in expanded ways: in the ordinary, the routine, even the simplest events of daily living. Elijah and Ambrose call us to see the Eternal with "the mind and the soul"; similarly, the challenge families face is to see with depth perception, noticing the Divine at work in a variety of ways: earth-shaking, simple, and everything in between.

C. S. Lewis weaves both these insights together when he writes the following:

> We may ignore, but we can nowhere evade, the presence of God. The world is crowded with Him. He walks everywhere *incognito*. And the *incognito* is not always hard to penetrate. The real labour is . . . to come awake. Still more, to remain awake.
>
> (*Letters to Malcolm*, p. 75)

In this book we attempt to awaken families' awareness of God. We propose a model (cf. appendix 2) that opens the mind and the soul of families to look deeply within their daily exchanges and recognize God "incognito." In seeing all kinds of ordinary events with depth perception, families may be surprised to discover God in unexpected places: laundry rooms, gravesides, birthday parties, and the like.

To begin, we offer real stories from real families. Following each story is a section called Breaking Open the Story, which contains questions inviting personal reflection. The purpose of these questions is to help us "see" the story with depth perception and to lead us to deeply investigate our own similar experiences. To do this, simply recall your own personal experiences, trying to be present to your feelings and thoughts. Avoid becoming analytical in your responses to the questions.

The family stories we have received and share with you, along with the related questions we ask, will call forth feelings, memories, thoughts, associations, and even questions. Our experience and fervent hope is that this evocative process will open your eyes, thus enabling you to see your family experiences with a whole new depth. This type of seeing will not leave you as you are but will bring you to the possibility of growth. This evocative process will develop in you a sensitivity to the depth that is present within family events, creating the opportunity to discover God's presence in your family's past as well as its present. This is the power of storytelling, as commented on by Edward Hays:

> Stories, fairy tales, and parables have always been the keys to open doorways that reason or logic cannot budge; for stories hold magic, and it is this element that unlocks the gates of wisdom and the human heart. . . .
>
> In ancient India, stories were given as medicine for anyone sick of heart or mind.
>
> *(Twelve and One-Half Keys*, back cover)

Some of these stories and the "breaking open" of them will evoke an awareness of blessings, while others may evoke painful memories. God constantly speaks to us through feelings and thoughts (both positive and negative). Therefore, when the story or questions surface a recognition of blessings in your life, we encourage you to take a moment to pray out of genuine gratitude for that which happened within your family and for the gift of seeing now with depth perception (cf. appendix 3).

When the story or questions surface painful memories, we invite you to take this hurt to God in prayer, now trusting in God's desire and power to heal you (cf. appendix 3). We believe that we only remember what we can deal with at any one time in our history. Consequently God is working with and through these evoked experiences to bring us (and possibly our families) to healing and wholeness. Trust that whatever emerges can be dealt with in the presence of God. Be assured that you will discover what you need to know; you will be given the grace and strength to move forward. After all, family spirituality is rooted in a broad range of experiences, from rich blessings to puzzling, painful times. Whether in gratitude or in pain, God is present and working within all areas of family life.

After each story is told and broken open, we offer insights that flow from the story. We realize that each story could be reflected on in a variety of ways, with multiple meanings, but we offer just one example, describing God's presence and work in that family at that time. Quite possibly you will find other meanings when you begin to see more than meets the eye.

A word of caution: There is a temptation to read this book quickly, that is, to browse through the family stories and scan the More Than Meets the Eye section for an insight or two that resonates with your own experience. In and of itself, this is not bad; however, this book is not meant to be read in one sitting. To develop "new eyes" (Marcel Proust) that see with depth perception, time is an essential ingredient. Therefore, we provide a final section, Rituals and Prayer. This last part of the process is purposely meant to slow you down, inviting you to "sip" and "savor," like fine wine, each family event, along with your own recollections. Depth perception is borne of such timely savoring.

The real power of ritual and prayer lies in its ability to bridge what you see with secular eyes with what you see through the eyes of faith. Such power suspends busyness and mental gymnastics, bringing you into a quiet, contemplative space. Thus forged by reflection (Breaking Open the Story) and prayer (Rituals and Prayer), God, who sustains, heals, and wonderfully transforms, can be encountered. Borrowing from the wisdom of Sr. Wendy Beckett, these family stories and this process "will only work to the extent that we wish them to work. If we fear the truth, if we are essentially reluctant to see what we have innocently hidden from ourselves, then nothing can open our eyes" (*The Gaze of Love*, p. 26).

The stories in this book—from friends, peers, and our own lives—were chosen for two purposes: to demonstrate a process of seeing with depth perception, and to witness the presence of God amid any and every event within family life. Consequently these are stories about special and routine occurrences, significant and trivial exchanges, young and old people, nuclear and extended families, and joys and sorrows. In these stories God's presence is sometimes loud and clear, but more often God's presence is soft and mysterious. Walk through the stories slowly, and "stay awake," discovering the riches of your own family's life. Otherwise life will go on, but opportunities to learn of God will be missed, revelation will go unnoticed.

Living artfully, therefore, might require something as simple as pausing. Some people are incapable of being arrested by things because they are always on the move. A common symptom of modern life is that there is no time for thought, or even for letting impressions of a day sink in. Yet it is only when the world enters the heart that it can be made into soul. The vessel in which soul-making takes place is an inner container scooped out by reflection and wonder.

(Thomas Moore, *Care of the Soul*, p. 286)

The chapter themes in this book are rooted in the following procla-mation of Pope John Paul II:

Hence the family has the mission to guard, reveal and communicate love, and this is a living reflection of and a real sharing in God's love for humanity and the love of Christ the Lord for the church, his bride. . . . The recent synod emphasized four general tasks for the family:
1. Forming a community of persons;
2. Serving life;
3. Participating in the development of society;
4. Sharing in the life and mission of the church.

(*Familiaris Consortio*, no. 17)

CHAPTER 1

Forming Community

Of all the tasks families are called on to perform, surely the most important one is building within each member a basic sense of identity and belonging. Throughout life a person will associate with no other group that can provide this critical function as profoundly as one's family.

Every community, from bowling teams to parish committees, has conditions for membership. Only the family strives to gather its members in an environment of unconditional love. Of course, God alone is fully capable of such unique love. As imitators, families struggle to create this intimacy through their daily living. In this way the experience of the home is a reflection—sometimes clear and sometimes fuzzy—of the unconditional love of God.

THE STORY TOLD Birthdays

O ur family always gets together for birthday parties: aunts, uncles, cousins, Grandma. Mom bakes a cake. The "birthday boy" is led into a darkened kitchen now aglow with candles on his cake. All voices come together as "Happy Birthday" is sung. Before the lights come back on, the year-older person blows out the candles, sometimes with the help of the little kids. Ice cream and cake is served, presents are opened, cameras flash.

When Brian (now ten years old) was having his third birthday party, we were all sitting around the living room. It was April 8th, and a thunderstorm had come up from the west. We had the west door and windows open. Just as Brian bent over to pick up a toy, an exceptionally bright flash of lightning struck. Brian immediately straightened up and said, "God took a picture of me." This is especially funny because Brian, being our first child, definitely had his picture taken a number of times.

> We who have rationalized our way out of the symbolic world often forget how to allow simple objects or actions to become the container of the sacred. Incarnation is the flesh-taking of the sacred.
> (Gertrud Mueller Nelson, *To Dance with God*, p. 33)

Breaking Open the Story

Rituals focus attention on what is most important. On this day it was Brian, but not just Brian. With family ritual, something bigger than ourselves is often experienced: the bonding among family members. The routine of leading the birthday boy into the kitchen, singing, blowing out the candles, and picture-taking offers everyone an experience of who they really are.

♦ Identify some of the ritual celebrations and traditions of your family. As you reflect, what does each reveal as most important to your family?

More Than Meets the Eye

Brian's birthday party is an example of good family ritual. Think for a few moments about the elements of ritual shown here. First, the party was sensual: we are "em-bodied" people; we experience through our senses. "Happy Birthday" being sung (hearing), a darkened kitchen aglow with candles (sight), ice cream and cake (taste), the birthday boy being led in (touch), and undoubtedly the scent of smoke when candles are blown out (smell)—all contributed to the experience of this family's birthday celebration. Family rituals are real: touchable, hearable, tastable, smellable, visual experiences!

Another element in building good family ritual is the setting. Parts of this birthday ritual took place in different rooms of Brian's home: the kitchen had its goings-on, the living room its activities. Where families gather is just as important as what happens there. Within each room, set activities happened: the birthday boy was led into the kitchen, there was movement to another place, and so on. Places, patterned movements, and gestures with special objects all contribute to building memorable family traditions.

Family rituals create an atmosphere of acceptance, belonging, and yet uniqueness. Brian's birthday party celebrated these realities. No family member gathered that April 8th would have said, "We are having a party to show Brian that he is a child of God." Yet the "holy," the "God-in-their-midst," did in fact show forth. Even at the age of three, Brian somehow felt a deep connection: his family's attention was also God's attention to him. In Brian's simple, child-like way, he was able to say, "God took my picture."

The best of family rituals feature engaging activities performed in patterned, sensual ways in specific places by a people gathered in common purpose. The value of such "good-habited" rituals is threefold: they build family ties, increase the personal worth of every individual, and open up God's presence.

Praying

For this prayer ritual, matches and a candle are needed. The candle should not be a votive, but rather a birthday candle or something similar.

1. Take two minutes to calm yourself and open a space for God. Sit comfortably, close your eyes, and focus your attention on your breathing for these moments, so that you may relax.

2. With eyes closed recall the details of your favorite birthday. Re-enter and relive this special birthday memory.

3. Answer this question: Why do I remember this particular birthday in such vivid detail; what made it memorable?

4. Express thanks to God for the people who were present in your recollections. For example, "Thank you, God, for _____, who . . ."

5. Open your eyes, light the candle, and spend a moment or two watching the flame. (Fire has long been a symbol of transformation, for it can reduce to ash as well as refine away impurities.)

6. Close your eyes again and compose a "wish of blessing" for a special person. You might begin by completing the following statement: "Loving God, I wish . . . for _____."

7. Blow out the candle, smelling the smoke brought about by your breath, the breath of life, God's life in you. Continue your day.

If this ritual is to be done with a group, the leader asks each person to find a personal space for prayer, then invites whomever wishes, to share their prayer experience and birthday memories with another person in the group.

THE STORY TOLD Graveside Thanksgiving

After my first husband, Bill, died, Anthony (my seven-year-old son) and I would visit the cemetery and spend some time there. When I remarried I was a little uncertain how my second husband, John, would respond to this tradition. It was John who suggested that he would like to take us to visit Bill. When we reached the graveside, we stood there silently. Anthony placed his flowers on the grave, and then John put his arms around both of us and prayed: "Thank you, Bill, for the gift of Mary and Anthony. I shall always take care of them."

> After the incarnation, we know that we are to look for God not in timeless glimpses of an angelic eternity, but at particular moments in particular places with their smells and sights, even places like Golgotha.
>
> (William L. Portier, *Tradition and Incarnation*, pp. 201–202)

Breaking Open the Story

At the heart of family spirituality is the interweaving of people and their lives. The family is constantly forming itself as a unit, as well as forming each individual member. Risking vulnerability, Mary and Anthony share their past pain with John.

- When have you risked being vulnerable by sharing your pain with another?
- How did sharing your pain with another affect your relationship?

In this story John responds to Mary and Anthony with reverence and gratitude.

- How might another person bring comfort to your situation?

More Than Meets the Eye

Mary and Anthony are carrying the pain of Bill's death. They could choose to wall themselves in with their pain, allowing any resentments and anger to fester and grow. Or they could choose to ignore the pain through denial. But in this instance, Mary and Anthony have opened themselves outward, allowing John to enter and become a part of their pain.

As a result of their risk taking, a next step becomes possible. John enters with a sense of gratitude. He might have come with a feeling of inferiority (Who am I to share this memory when I wasn't even there?), an attitude of superiority (What's wrong with them? Let the past go; it's long gone.), or even fear at being the new husband and father. John chooses to be thankful for his wife and son and thankful in particular for Bill and his effect in their lives.

John's prayer of gratitude and his embrace enflesh God's comfort for Mary and Anthony. Gratitude has the potential to transform situations, even the most painful or evil ones, by reframing them. In being grateful for their past, John enables them to recognize God in the present, even in their pain. When asked about it later, Mary reflected on this incident, saying, "John's prayer of thanksgiving spoke of our gratitude to a God who had walked with us in our pain as well as in our joy."

The combination of shared grief and gratitude strengthened the bonds among the members of this new family. Together these three people shared a moment of genuine intimacy. When family members enter both the light and dark moments of one another's lives, intimacy grows and God is made manifest.

Praying

Before beginning this ritual, find a photo of a deceased loved one: a spouse, parent, child, grandparent, sibling, intimate friend . . . whomever you wish. (Special people touch us deeply, and often their pictures become "family icons," which remind us of their sacredness in our life.)

1. Sit comfortably with this photo resting in your lap. With your eyes closed, take some gentle breaths to relax yourself.

2. Open your eyes, pick up your family icon, and gaze at the person who is so loved. Let your mind wander to that person's life and your shared times. Enjoy the flood of memories.

3. Recognize and acknowledge any sadness that you still feel about losing this person.

4. Place the photo on the floor in front of you where you can still see it, then sit back. There is separation and distance because of death, yet a nearness and oneness remains. Staying in this position, pray the following words slowly and calmly at least three times:

Loving God,
thank you for _____;
thank you for her [or him] being in my life!
Thank you for our times together,
including this moment with our memories.
May _____ be enjoying eternal life with you;
may I join you both when my days on this earth end.
Amen.

In a group setting, one person serves as leader, bringing the family icon to the group. The leader asks the others to recall "in their mind's eye" a treasured photo of someone now deceased. The leader models for them the rite of placing the photo on the floor; all others do so in their imagination. The leader then may ask all to share their reflections with at least one other person in the group.

THE STORY TOLD Sibling Rivalry

I have been a single parent for over twenty years, starting when my children were ages three, two, and one. One of the most difficult situations for me to deal with was the ongoing sibling rivalry between my two sons. They really had a terrible case. I know that I felt guilty and angry that they didn't have a father to help them deal with "male stuff" and each other. The tension decreased when one of them entered the service and was away from home.

It wasn't until after the Christmas holidays one year that the two of them were able to—or forced to—spend some time together, and they treated each other as responsible, caring adults. We were all sitting together at the dinner table, and they began to talk about their fierce fights and laugh about them. I was even able to share how responsible I felt for them and their fighting and how worried I used to feel. All the prayers I had prayed for them had not been unheard (although with my fragile trust, I often wondered), and we established a new family relationship with one another—an adult one based on today. We also welcomed a new brother into our family—my daughter's husband.

We had come together to a new place, very different from the struggle of growing up, but very much still a family. The bond is there even though each has his or her own life. I thank God for that, for their reaching adulthood, and for my sanity through it all!

> All of us, at times, feel like Jesus did in the tomb. We're tempted to believe that God has abandoned us whenever we feel the absence in our life of the Presence. Our greatest moments, the ones that call forth greatness from deep within us, usually happen when we feel totally abandoned yet still cling to that thread that's thinner than a hair.
>
> (Edward Hays, *The Magic Lantern*, p. 144)

Breaking Open the Story

Family life is far from clean and tidy. On a regular basis, we experience the messiness and pain of living and growing up together. Amid such conflicts is the temptation to think that this struggle will never end and that we have failed.

♦ As you recall instances of conflict or frustration in your family, what were the temptations you faced?

♦ There is a certain movement in this story, namely, that difficult moments can bring us to "a new place, very different from the struggle," which is in fact a better place. How has time given you a different perspective on any of your family conflicts or frustrations?

More Than Meets the Eye

This mother finally sees her boys' rivalry in the context of their growth to adulthood. For twenty years she had to deal with the very real temptation to narrow her vision, to measure the worth of her children and her own effectiveness as a parent by what she could see on any given day, week, or month.

Family has a history, and not all parts of that history look positive. In the broad sweep of things, individual moments and phases (though sometimes frustrating) demonstrate that families are challenged to see with breadth perception. Breadth perception is recognizing and placing a particular moment within the context of history. Breadth perception allows a sower to see the seed at every stage of its development, from sprouting to yielding fruit. Just as each seed has a cycle of growth, so too does the family.

Within this family the fighting between brothers is one phase in the ongoing history of their development. Just as the seed is not judged until harvest, so too the relationship of these brothers is not to be judged solely on their adolescent sibling rivalry. Breadth perception allows a parent to see an adolescent as an unfinished creation, and to be patient and faithful to the process going on in that child. This mother was faithful to what she was sowing, continuing to pray in "fragile trust" to God, with whom she co-parents.

Praying

No objects are needed in this prayer exercise, just your hands.

1. Be seated with your hands resting in your lap. Close your eyes and concentrate on your breathing. Feel your chest rising and falling from within, feel the air moving through your nostrils. . . . Become calm.

2. With your eyes still closed, lift your hands a few inches above your lap and begin to move your fingers, slowly, rhythmically. Stretch them, flex them, go through a whole range of movements, experiencing your hands from within.

3. Feel one hand with the other, eyes still closed. Feel your calluses, knuckles, and any other distinguishing features of your hands.

4. Consider how your hands have worked:
- the blisters from raking
- the paper cuts from envelopes
- the soreness from gripping heavy, awkward things
- the scrapes from kitchen knives . . .

all accomplishments by your hands.

5. Consider how your hands have been expressions of your care for others:
- the tear thumbed away (someone else's or even your own)
- the cupping of a child's face
- the neck rubs for a tired spouse
- the strong handshakes of friendship . . .

all services by your hands.

6. But consider now how your hands have hurt:
- the wagging index finger of anger
- the clenched fist
- the pokes and jabs to someone's chest
- the slap of violence . . .

all pains caused by your hands.

7. Place both hands on your heart and press gently until you begin to feel the beating within. (Hands often become the outward expression of inner thoughts and emotions.)

8. Can you feel in your heart some family member who may be hurting? Does any family member need your hands in help? Are tasks that might benefit your family still undone?

9. Choose one person, thought, or project that has risen within you and resolve to heal it, labor at it, help it, or caress it, all with your hands!

If this ritual is done in a group, one person may serve as a leader and read the instructions for the others. At the end the leader invites all who wish to, to share their resolve to heal, labor, help, or caress.

THE STORY TOLD Gram and Grampa

We started going to church on Saturday night when our children were small. After church we stopped at Gram and Grampa's house. Gram would be ready with freshly popped popcorn, games to play, coloring books, and stories to read. While Gram was constantly on the go trying to please, Grampa sat in his chair and watched and teased the baby, who always had to be laid on the sofa beside his chair. Later we sat at the kitchen table and ate ice cream and angel food cake and drank pop and coffee. (Sunday dinners frequently had Gram bringing dill pickles, strawberry preserves, and other goodies from her cellar.) It is hard to figure out whether the grandparents or the grandchildren had a better time.

The older kids still talk about these special nights. The two youngest children will never experience these special nights, but they enjoy the stories the older ones tell of them.

> All guests who present themselves are to be welcomed as Christ.
> (Timothy Fry, editor, *The Rule of St. Benedict in English*, p. 73)

Breaking Open the Story

What happened that made these nights so memorable, so special to this family? While Gram couldn't do enough for the grandchildren, plying them with popcorn, angel food cake, games, and all, Grampa couldn't be more totally present to them. On these Saturday nights, the "being with" and "doing for" created hospitality.

- ♦ Recall a time when you extended this type of hospitality, or received it. Describe who was present and what was done. It is evident that these grandparents took sheer delight in their grandchildren. Where have you experienced such delight?
- ♦ How might these occasions of hospitality and delight be an experience of God for you?

More Than Meets the Eye

This family's first Saturday ritual took place at the parish church: gathering, hearing the stories of salvation, breaking and sharing bread, and all the other "routines" of Mass. These opened this family to the deeper reality of God's presence in their midst.

The extravagant love of these grandparents invited all to enter a second ritual: the warm welcome; the familiar rooms; the food, games, seating; and the storytelling (passing on of tales from one generation to the next). Through their extravagant love, these grandparents revealed the face of God to their grandchildren. They anticipated their family's arrival with much preparation. They had a constant desire and readiness to please, and a joy in watching their grandchildren enjoy themselves. The fact that "Gram was constantly on the go trying to please . . ." created an environment of hospitality the entire family enjoyed. The root of the word *hospitality* is connected with "guest room." True hospitality is possible only when we open the guest rooms of our heart to others. The ministry of hospitality, done so clearly by these grandparents, transformed such ordinary things as popcorn and ice cream into experiences of communion.

The author of the Letter to the Hebrews knew this well when stating the following:

> Let mutual love continue. Do not neglect to show hospitality to strangers, for by doing that some have entertained angels without knowing it.
>
> (Hebrews 13:1–2)

In extending hospitality, it's not only what is shared that matters but also the spirit in which the sharing takes place. In this story it's a spirit of pure delight, so much so that it becomes difficult to figure out who has the better time, grandchildren or grandparents. Such simple delight is an imitation of our God's extravagant love for us. "The LORD takes pleasure in his people" (Psalm 149:4), or again, "But you shall be called My Delight Is in Her . . . for the

LORD delights in you" (Isaiah 62:4). Just imagine, the hospitality of these delighted grandparents mirrors God's delight with all people.

The hospitality of the grandparents, shown with an awareness of "entertaining angels," made ordinary, small events genuine entry points into the sacred.

Praying

Delight (de-lit'), *v.t.* to gratify or please greatly; charm: *v.i.* be highly gratified or pleased (with in): *n.* an extreme degree of pleasure; high satisfaction; joy.
(*Webster's New School and Office Dictionary,* 1958)

1. Select a piece of music, a photo, a painting, a sculpture, or the like, that absolutely delights you.

2. Get into a relaxed and comfortable position so you can enjoy this favored piece for a while. Take a few deep breaths. . . . Calm yourself as much as possible.

3. Listen to the music or gaze on the piece you've selected. Let the experience wash over you fully. Let your mind free-flow to whatever images it unconsciously wishes to surface for you.

4. In this time of associations, pause with each image to take delight in what it speaks. For example, you might recall:
- a person now deceased
- a hurt from a time when you argued while this music was playing
- the silence on a long drive when this piece came on the radio
- a discussion of where to hang this print in a new home, as opposed to the former home

Spend a few moments with whatever rises in you.

5. Mentally and spiritually transition yourself to this truth: God does the same with your life! God sees you and absolutely delights in you! God might recall:
- the time you called out in sheer joy
- the care you gave to your flu-ridden child

- an insight you gained through the Scriptures
- you reading this book now, and opening yourself to God's gift of remembrances
- God delighting in you!

6. Breathe deeply, with eyes closed, and revel in the fact that the LORD delights in you" (Isaiah 62:4).

In a group setting, the leader should select a piece of music beforehand, making arrangements so that it may be heard by all. The leader will then guide the group through the ritual experience.

THE STORY TOLD Wondering Why

For all practical purposes, I lost my family in 1975, after both my parents died, but I did not really realize it until 1992. At that time, after twenty years of teaching, I was burned out and had decided to change professions. I chose real estate. Evidently, to my family this was a cardinal sin. During the first year I was in real estate, I was in contact with my family five times—and all five times were initiated by me. Even at Thanksgiving and Christmas, only one sister-in-law invited me to dinner, one day before the holiday. By that time I had already accepted an invitation from my broker and his wife to share the holidays with them and their family. It was an extremely lonely year!

This exclusion has persisted to the present time. I do not hear from any of my brothers or my sister living here in town unless I initiate the contact. Usually when I do call my sister, it is obvious from the tone of her voice that she is not interested in carrying on a conversation. I have had several surgeries in the past eight years, and after one of them, I was laid up for a period of two months. My sister came to visit me once while I was hospitalized, and a niece came to drive me home from the hospital, but that was the only contact with my family living here. When I had a hip replacement, my sister came to wait while I was in surgery and came to visit me once. I was hospitalized for eight days, and that was the only contact I had with my family during that time. I did receive a bouquet of flowers from one niece.

Holidays come and go, and except for Christmas, Easter, and Thanksgiving, I usually spend them completely alone. On these major holidays, I spend time with a nephew and his family or, at the last minute, one sister-in-law calls to invite me for dinner.

I have spent many, many lonely days and nights during these years and have shed buckets of tears, wondering why.

One day in group, as I struggled not to break down under the weight of knowing that my primary caregivers were not capable of giving me care, this Catholic nun gently reached over and touched

my hand. Who knows at what point of discouragement and de-
spair the simplest act of love may reach a soul and turn it again to
the light? This simple act of love taught me that my family of origin
might never be there for me, but in the providence of God many
others have been sent to reach out and to touch my life with love,
concern, compassion, and care.

(Linda H. Hollies, "A Daughter Survives Incest," in *Double Stitch*,
edited by Patricia Bell-Scott et al., pp. 160–161)

Breaking Open the Story

Feelings of belonging and acceptance are assumed when thinking
of family. Yet in this story loneliness and rejection are the realities.

+ In what ways have you experienced loneliness and rejection
from your family of origin?
+ During these times of loneliness and rejection, where did
you experience belonging and acceptance?
+ Thinking back, can you now use these experiences of alienation to discover something about God?

More Than Meets the Eye

Biological families do not always provide the experience of intimate
community desired by their members. Even though family members
have shared common events, ancestors, experiences—in short, have
a long history together—sometimes these same people become
alienated. The result is loneliness and pain.

But wisdom can be found while wrestling with this kind of
suffering. For believers the process of healing begins by transforming the question "Why is God doing this to me?" to the faith-filled
question, "How is God already working within this?" Even as she
makes efforts to reconcile with her biological family, this storyteller
may discover love and acceptance in other guises, for example,
with the real estate broker who invited her to dinner.

We need to remember that God provides more than one family
for all of us. Intimate community may be found within the larger

human family, with those who are "othersisters," "otherbrothers," "otherfathers," and "othermothers." (These terms are adapted from "Turbulence and Tenderness," by Rosalie Riegle Troester, in *Double Stitch,* p. 163.)

The experience of intimate belonging is in fact an experience of God.

Praying

First, relax in the presence of God. Sit comfortably in a straight-backed chair with your hands resting in your lap. Breathe deeply, being aware of the air moving in and out of your lungs, your chest rising and falling. By focusing all your attention on this simple act, many of the other distractions and concerns of the day may fall away.

1. Cup your hands, still resting them in your lap. Now imagine in your hands whatever is currently causing you suffering; look at it from different angles until you can almost feel it.

2. Lift your hands high and consciously give this cause of your suffering to God.

3. Return your hands to a normal level, still cupped, and speak aloud, "Give me what you want to give me."

4. Sit for a few moments in this posture of acceptance.

5. Close your prayer by repeating aloud several times, "My refuge and my fortress; / my God, in whom I trust" (Psalm 91:2).

6. As you leave this time of reflection, form a phrase or sentence that summarizes what God has given to you. In the course of your day, try to recall and reaffirm God's gift.

If praying with a group, the leader guides the others by speaking aloud each step, then pausing sufficiently so that all may reflect. When step 5 is reached, invite the group members to close their eyes while the leader begins gently to repeat the psalm verse until all have joined in.

THE STORIES TOLD Shared Chores

Summer meant Sunday picnics for my household. All four of us would often go to the earliest Mass on Sunday morning (pre–Vatican II, no anticipated Saturday liturgies). Then the tasks would begin. Mom would start peeling and cubing the cooked potatoes (boiled the night before so as to be cooled and ready); Dad, with his large mechanic's hands, cracked, peeled, and chopped the hard-boiled eggs; that left my brother and me on various vegetables—shredding, slicing, and dicing carrots, radishes, green peppers, and my favorite, the sweet pickles! When those were shredded, the kitchen was filled with their aroma. Ah, the scraped knuckles of Sunday mornings on the vegetable shredder!

As each item was finished, it was dumped into the largest bowl in the house, a lidded Tupperware jobber. No matter how many times the final mixing took place, we rarely were absent: globs of mayonnaise spooned in, squirts of mustard, shakes of pepper, paprika . . . how anything so unmeasured could blend so well is still a mystery. The delights that wooden mixing spoon brought. Then, the ritual tasting! Each of us held a teaspoon in hand, waiting for Mom's nod. "It needs more . . ." "Don't you think we should add . . ." "We forgot the . . ." And ending invariably with "It'll be better yet when it's cold!"

I can smell the moist black earth just thinking about it. Early in spring we would pack up buckets and spades, pile into the car, and drive to Carter Lake Park. It was an early morning ritual that included the whole family plus Grandma, who lived next door.

The park was still empty and the lake calm like a smooth blue mirror. It was a race to see who could find and dig up the greenest, leafiest chicotia plants, not the large tough ones but those with tender shoots that went into salads, were boiled like spinach, or were frozen for later use in soup.

We ran from spot to spot until our buckets were full, and then played too close to the bank of the lake while Mom, Dad, and Grandma finished the job of shaking off excess dirt and trimming tough stems.

Back home the kitchen sink was filled with water and each plant was soaked and cleaned in assembly-line fashion. Each bunch was cut and put in plastic bread sacks that Mother had washed and saved for this purpose.

I never really liked the taste of the leafy green treasures we hunted on those crisp, sunny mornings, but I still remember those times of communal harvesting.

It was late summer, and the pullets would soon be laying eggs. This was a favorite time of the year for me, for it was time to gather the pullets from the freedom of the outdoors and place them into their new permanent home, the chicken coop. And this was a task that required the entire family, even Cookie, our loyal rat terrier.

We ate supper early, then waited for the sun to set, because that was the clock for the pullets. Toward nightfall they would prepare for sleep by gathering in the small pullet house and in the trees. We had to catch the pullets, carry them to the chicken coop, vaccinate them, and debeak them for their permanent residence as egg layers.

All six of us worked together to catch and carry the pullets to the cage outside the chicken coop. Cookie's job was to catch the birds that seemed to have more pheasant than domestic chicken blood in them. Cookie was a natural at running down the wild ones and holding them, without harm, until one of us removed the chicken from his grasp.

When the cage was filled outside the chicken coop, we shifted gears. The taller kids would reach into the cage and hand the chickens to the younger kids, who held them just right for our mother to vaccinate them. Then we handed the frightened young birds to my father, who had the task of debeaking them. I was most fascinated by this; I never seemed quite able to master the way of getting the pullet to open her mouth so that the upper beak could be cut to protect her neighbors from harmful pecking. After Dad debeaked each bird, it was released into its new home, the larger chicken coop.

As I recall those nights, it was a time when the regular schedule of work, supper, showers, homework, and bedtime was altered. It was exciting going out into the night as a family, tackling a job as though we were one. Even Cookie was a valuable unit in the family. It was a night when there was little fighting and competition among my siblings. We were a team, working for our livelihood.

> A home is meant to provide more than nocturnal storage units for isolated individuals who spend most of the day going their own ways. Rather, it must house a deep affective network of people who choose to gift each other with their caring presence. To build a family into a community where life and love are joyfully shared requires hard work and commitment.
>
> (Wilkie Au, *By Way of the Heart,* p. 50)

Breaking Open the Stories

These are obviously pleasant memories: these occasions were fun! Why? There's energy created when common tasks are done in a ritual way. That energy flows from the experience of community, wherein individual members have a great feeling of belonging to one another.

If one person was to make potato salad alone, or pick enough greens for a season by herself, or debeak hundreds of chickens solo, the task would seem long and tedious. When every member of a family works together, contributing however much or little each is capable of, the task gets accomplished more easily.

In addition, the higher goal of binding family members together is achieved.

- ♦ Identify tasks your family has completed together.
- ♦ To what extent have you experienced this higher goal of being bound together?

♦ What might this experience of belonging with your family reveal to you about belonging to God?

More Than Meets the Eye

For longer than history can recall, one of the strengths of family has been that it works together as a unit to accomplish necessary tasks. Each of these stories depicts an ordinary task being accomplished. But the focus of these stories is on the whole family working together as a unit. Diverse personalities, with differing likes, dislikes, moods, and stages of development, all blend to form a unique whole, far beyond the sum of the parts. Family is often the first setting in which we experience such unity and oneness.

This experience is sacramental for believers. That is, experiences of intimate community within family give a glimpse of our oneness as the Body of Christ. "For just as the body is one and has many members, and all the members of the body, though many, are one body, so it is with Christ" (1 Corinthians 12:12).

At times families live Paul's insight. As these stories describe, each member of the family appears unique, distinct, and separate from one another. Yet at the same time, there is a deeper communion or union between and among them than their apparent distinctiveness. Paul uses this experience to explain our oneness in Christ. And Paul's most significant message is the truth that we are more deeply united as one than we are separate.

Moments when we notice this oneness within family can be moments of glimpsing the divine communion God has with us in Christ.

Praying

In this technological age, our society has become terribly individualistic, leaving many of us feeling isolated and lonely. The church has taken a countercultural stance, one that challenges parents, by word and example, to be "the first heralds of the faith with regard to their children" (Vatican Council II, *Dogmatic Constitution on the Domestic Church,* no. 11). The Council went so far as to call family "the Domestic Church," a term that recognizes the family as the most basic unit of both society and the church itself.

Therefore, we need to be creative in planning occasions to work together, tasks and times when we can experience the true oneness we have been called to as family.

1. Plan a common activity for your family, no matter how that family is currently shaped. It might be a communal task, such as cleaning the garage or washing your "domestic church" windows, inside and out.

2. Or find and make a special recipe handed down from generation to generation going back to the "old country." It probably hasn't been made for years because "it takes so long."

3. Perhaps you've had some seasonal project in mind that your family has never done before, but that could easily become an annual tradition for you. Good ideas in this category include:

- caroling (Are you aware that the Christmas season doesn't end until the Baptism of the Lord, usually the second Sunday of January?)
- a Fourth of July picnic
- a progressive dinner among extended family
- luminarias around your property
- hosting a neighborhood card party

The possibilities are really limitless.

All that is needed for these family experiences is a convener, one who will initiate, orchestrate, and delegate the necessary parts and pieces. You can be that convener this time, the one who calls the others together. So get out some paper and a pen and begin writing answers to these questions:

- What shall we do?
- Who will participate?
- When and where will this event take place?
- What items and skills are needed?

Once you've answered the questions, take a deep breath and brace yourself for some opposition. Individuals may balk and complain, so keep a good sense of humor—but be persistent. Affirm and praise the cooperation and effort; ignore the complaints.

If you are meeting with a group for this ritual, you may wish to engage in some communal task right now. When all are finished, gather in a circle, holding hands, each praying silently for a moment, and then speak or sing the following:

> We are many parts, we are all one body,
> and the gifts we have we are given to share.
> May the Spirit of love make us one indeed;
> one, the love that we share, one, our hope in despair,
> one, the cross that we bear.
>
> (Marty Haugen, "We Are Many Parts")

THE STORY TOLD Dying Young

Eighteen is too young to die. Matt's body, neatly dressed in the suit he bought for graduation, lay flat with hands folded . . . so out of character for a boy who thought brakes on a go-cart were an accessory and fences merely jumping posts. He wasn't my son, though he jumped our fences and drove our go-carts. But he could have been our son—or anyone's. Despite frequent warnings from his parents not to drink and drive, Matt's car hit a power pole at seventy-five miles per hour. His blood test showed that he had been drinking heavily prior to the accident. The family was able to donate his organs to patients awaiting transplants.

Seeing Matt's face in the casket and remembering his infectious smile made me think about how fragile human life is.

> Oh, only for so short a while
> you have loaned us to each other,
> because we take form in your act of drawing us,
> and we take life in your painting us,
> and we breathe in your singing us.
> But only for so short a while
> have you loaned us to each other.
>
> (An ancient Aztec Indian prayer, quoted in *Praying Our Goodbyes*, by Joyce Rupp, p. 69)

Breaking Open the Story

Eighteen is too young to die! How difficult for a parent to bury a child. Of all the reactions this mother-friend shared, from tears and anger to questions and second-guessing, her feelings led her to a truth: how fragile human life really is!

Recall a time when you were aware of the fragility of life.

- ♦ How did you respond to that situation?
- ♦ How did that experience affect your relationship with God?

More Than Meets the Eye

Life is so fragile, and Matt's death is vivid testimony to this fact. From the first moment of conception, parents begin to develop attitudes and habits by which they deal with the fragility of the life given them. They learn to nurture, guard, support, and care for those they love. On the one hand, they may be tempted to overprotect, even control; on the other hand, parents also may be tempted to give up, even abandon their child. Healthy parenting seeks a balance between these two extremes—being protective while at the same time encouraging a child to stand on his or her own. For example, Matt's parents cautioned him, but they could not prevent the tragic consequences of his choice to drive after drinking.

Nevertheless, Matt's parents, or any parents, are not the first to be faced with this balance. The history of salvation is filled with examples of how God has never forced us into what may be best (control), nor ever abandoned us. God's ways could be described as a letting-go love. It is unconditional and always, a love that remains constant even though it may not be returned. It is openhanded, always giving help while respecting our freedom.

Holy parenting seeks to walk the same line as God, "gracefully" nurturing and encouraging without demanding or forsaking. In imitation of God's ways, holy parenting calls for a love that also lets go. Parental love offers guidance and sets limits while respecting a child's freedom. It creates a respectful space filled with unconditional love. The ability to love in this way is a lifelong process.

When faced with the fragility of life, parents are challenged to take a stance of trust in God, whose love for their child(ren) far exceeds their own.

Praying

For this ritual time, it would be helpful to have a recent picture of your family. If none is available, try drawing a picture of each member in your mind's eye

1. Be seated comfortably, and with your eyes closed, begin to breathe deeply, focusing your attention on your own breath . . . the "ru'ah Yahweh," the "breath of God" without which there is no life.

2. If you have a photo of your family, open your eyes and look closely at each member; if your picture is in your mind, keep your eyes closed, but call each member to mind separately.

3. Start with your oldest child, and contemplate him or her for a few moments. Make the following statements of belief in God's parental care:

- Lord, I believe that you gave this child to me as a gift.
- I know that you love my child, _____, unconditionally.
- I feel helpless with my child when . . .
- I give my child to you.
- Thank you for your ever present protection and care.

4. Repeat this pattern for each of your children.

5. Draw your prayer time to a close by again sitting quietly, breathing deeply. The same "ru'ah Yahweh" animating your life is also active in the lives of your children.

When praying in a group setting, the leader invites all to form in their mind a clear picture of each family member. Proceed only when this is done. The leader asks the participants to repeat each line of the prayer words found in step 3, pausing long enough for each to "fill in the blanks" aloud, whether it's with a name or a situation of helplessness.

THE STORY TOLD *Good-Night Kiss*

Each night on her way upstairs to bed, our daughter, Sarah, would race around the center hall stairway, make a beeline to the corner of the study where her dad sat in his recliner, and jump into his lap in a heap.

Head on his chest, they would "good-night kiss," and she would unload any unresolved troubles from the day . . . sometimes for only a few moments, at other times for long minutes.

> And a voice came from heaven, "You are my Son, the Beloved; with you I am well pleased."
>
> (Luke 3:22)

Breaking Open the Story

The complete attention of Sarah's dad during her nightly sharing left her feeling accepted, secure, and loved.

- ◆ Recall someone in your family from whom you receive such total attention. What is that like for you?
- ◆ In exchanges like this, both Sarah and her dad could explore, stretch, and mature in their understanding of who they each are. When someone is so attentive to you, in what ways does this shape you?

More Than Meets the Eye

No matter what filled her day, Sarah had someone special who gave her undivided attention. Even though her dad was not with her each moment of the day, he became her companion by listening to her stories. Though he couldn't erase the hurts or mishaps of the day, his attention now let Sarah know that she was not alone in facing them.

These exchanges of holding, listening, and speaking to one another are the ordinary ways a family communicates a sense of identity, worth, and belonging. In this sense the family is a place of ongoing formation for each member—all participating in the creation of the other. Words, glances, open ears and arms, are simple gestures that can say to us, You are loved, you are not alone, and you are one of us. By contrast, these same gestures misused (for example, criticism, sneers, closed ears and hearts) can de-form us. The result may be a false sense of identity, a feeling that you are not loved or accepted.

The assurance being communicated to Sarah on her father's lap is that she is beloved within her family. Such scenes make real for us the truth that we are also God's beloved. Messages like these are spoken by God to each of us throughout our life—not thundered from the clouds or sent on scrolls by angels, but delivered by the mouths and ears, arms and laps of those who love us.

A great consolation flowing from our identity as God's beloved is the knowledge that we are never alone in this life. Just as Sarah's dad listens to her stories daily, God is the one who listens, who holds our disappointments, celebrates our accomplishments, and works with us as our constant companion.

Praying

Who is present, who is with you at most times of your day, at least symbolically?

1. Get out your purse or billfold right now and open it. Whose pictures do you carry? Do you have a formal sitting of family, a treasured snapshot of a loved one, or just portraits of dead presidents on dollar bills?

2. If you have family photos, as you hold the pictures of your special people, take a few moments to raise all in prayer.

If you have no photos, rest your hands in your lap, shaping them like a cup, as if to hold each family member, and raise all in prayer.

3. With each person securely in your mind and your heart, pray all five of the following blessings slowly and meditatively.

- The first time through, pray for yourself, inserting "I" in each blank.

- After praying for yourself, insert the name of any person who is dear to you. Repeat the process as many times as you wish.
- When all individuals have been remembered, raise "our family" as you again pray each line twice.
- Finally, be sure to finish this blessing by praying for "all beings."

   May _____ be well, happy, and peaceful. (Repeat.)

   May _____ be free of pain and suffering in mind and
      body. (Repeat.)

   May _____ have ease of being in life. (Repeat.)

   May _____ accept my (their) life moment by moment.
      (Repeat.)

   May _____ come to union with God. (Repeat.)

   4. Rest quietly, without thinking, for a few moments before
returning to the rest of your day.

If you are doing this ritual in a group, one person can lead the others through the five blessing prayers. Have all close their eyes while sitting comfortably.

The leader speaks one line slowly and everyone repeats it twice, silently, in their own mind and heart. The leader continues with the next line, and so on.

When finished, sit quietly in the silence before moving on with the rest of the day.

———◆———

CHAPTER 2

Serving Life

Because every person is made in the image and likeness of God, each of us to some extent shares in God's power to create and sustain, or serve, life. In the experience of family, sharing in this power of God implies more than birthing or adopting children. Whenever one fulfills the ordinary tasks of feeding, clothing, and sheltering another, teaching right from wrong, guiding physical and intellectual growth, sharing the Good News of Jesus Christ, one is giving and serving life.

In addition to these actions, families are called to foster a healthy reverence for life in all its expressions: aged, infirm, unborn, persons of another color, and people who are physically or mentally challenged.

Reverence for life extends to all creation. Enjoying the simplest of earthworms to the most spectacular of sunsets can lead the family to both wonder and responsibility for all that is.

THE STORY TOLD Notes from a Mother's Diary

Tonight at bedtime Adam's prayer was: "Dear God, thank you for our new dishwasher. I love you, God; thank you for helping me when I need help."

Last Sunday, March 11, Adam found a little worm. He carried it around carefully, his "pet." When he put it down on the concrete, I suggested he better put it in the dirt or it would die. "Oh, yeah, I better," he said, "I don't think he's ready to go to heaven yet."

March 22, on the way to school one day:

Mom: "It will be fun to see your friends again this week."

Adam: "Yes, it will. And I'm very glad I'm myself."

> People of the earth. Attuned to the wisdom of life-giving humus, the patience of rocks, the dignity of trees and the essential contribution of each creeping-crawling thing, we come to know something of the divine milieu of which we are a part.
>
> (Wendy M. Wright, *Sacred Dwelling*, p. 194)

Breaking Open the Story

"Out of the mouths of babes . . . ." Little children do say the darndest things, from the hilarious to the most profound, all with utter simplicity.

♦ Remember times when you were inspired or challenged by the simplicity of a child.

Adam gives witness to what he "knows" to be the truth. Speculate for a moment:

♦ How could Adam's parents have instilled these basic beliefs in their child of four?

♦ If you are a parent, name some truths you wish to hand on to your child(ren). How are you attempting to share these truths?

More Than Meets the Eye

These diary excerpts of Adam are endearing, but they also demonstrate something quite profound. The entries imply that big ideas are active in Adam's young life. What his parents believe and how they live has begun to take root in Adam's life very early on. There's no doubt that his parents planted the truths of resurrection, thanksgiving, and self-esteem at an early age. They seem to know that most things about life, including faith and religion, are more "caught" than formally taught. Adam lives, breathes, and grows in this atmosphere.

The ordinary events of daily living become occasions wherein the teaching of great truths about God and life can happen, sometimes in the simplest ways. Matters of faith are shared in ordinary conversations about dishwashers and worms. When parents present the faith in simple and creative ways, wording difficult ideas in ways children can comprehend, "truth-passing" happens. For instance, on Sunday, March 11, Adam was able to say, "I don't think he (the worm) is ready to go to heaven yet." The cycle of birth-life-death is already understood by him at some very basic level. And in terms of faith, he has already been exposed to belief in resurrection.

In this process of truth-passing, parents grow just as much as their children. Adam gives back to his mother what she has given to him. His straightforward, simple witnessing with worms, thanksgiving, and sense of self preaches. His mother is touched so deeply that she reflects on and records his words in her diary. In the family the roles of teacher and learner are always fluid, changing quickly from parent to child, and vice versa.

These exchanges of truth-passing are holy because parents and children give and receive a word that feeds more than the body. It is important for parents to remain open to hearing God's voice coming from the mouth of their child, as they announce the Good News to him or her.

Praying

1. Place yourself in the presence of our God by sitting quietly, imaging your peaceful place, breathing deeply—whatever may be your practice for entering prayer.

2. Read the following story reflectively, more than once if it is helpful or necessary:

> The Master was an advocate both of learning and of Wisdom.
> "Learning," he said when asked, "is gotten by reading books or listening to lectures."
> "And Wisdom?"
> "By reading the book that is you."
> He added as an afterthought: "Not an easy task at all, for every minute of the day brings a new edition of the book!"
> (Anthony de Mello, *One Minute Wisdom*, p. 177)

3. Recall some addition to the personal book "that is you" during the past twenty-four hours. What feelings arise in you from this "new edition"? (Remember that feelings are often signs of something important going on inside us.)

4. As a result of these feelings, respond to God in some words of prayer: praise, repentance, a cry for help, and so on.

If this ritual is shared within a group, the leader may need to repeat aloud periodically the short encounter with the Master, so that its full impact may be gained. After sufficient time for individual reflection (in step 3), all may be asked to share in small groups the additions to the personal book "that is you." Then reminding all of the sacredness of hearing another person's prayer, invite the entire group to speak their praise, repentance, pleas for help, and so on, in closing.

THE STORY TOLD The Many Faces of Parenting

Because I was the oldest in a large Catholic family and had sixty-four first cousins, I had nothing in my life experience to prepare me for the sorrow and loneliness of my own infertility. Almost everyone I knew was part of a large family, and I was sure that God always blessed Irish Catholic women with many babies.

As the months and then the years began to go by, I found myself asking questions about why God was punishing us, why God would allow those who didn't want children to become pregnant, and so on. I moved through several emotional stages over and over again. Denial, anger, depression, rage, grief, hope, trust—all became my daily companions.

Occasionally we would think I might be pregnant, and then once again we would ride the emotional roller coaster until we would find out each time that it was a false alarm.

I do know that this experience of infertility was a bonding one for my husband and me. We learned many lessons about how to comfort, reassure, understand, and just be with each other in our shared pain and disappointment. We also learned to be more sensitive to other people who were experiencing any type of emotional turmoil. We knew the joy of having people in our lives who tried to understand, and we hoped to pass that on to others.

My husband and I were both teachers, so we began to find tremendous strength in our work with other people's children. It was probably our work with these students that began to call us to strongly explore the possibility of adoption. Could it be that God had a child somewhere for us?

Our prayer turned to a more inclusive vision of parenthood, and shortly after we made that conversion, our God blessed us with a miracle: a healthy, beautiful, brown-eyed, red-faced baby boy. He was even born on Valentine's Day, which we acknowledged as another gift from God. I prayed for the sixteen-year-old woman who courageously gave her robust new baby son to us in a powerful act of love and trust that was probably the most difficult thing she had

ever done in her short lifetime. I continue to pray for her today
. . . fourteen years later.

> The gloom of the world is but a shadow. Behind it, yet within reach,
> is joy.
> There is a radiance and glory in the darkness, could we but
> see, and to see, we have only to look. I beseech you to look.
>
> (Fra Giovanni, 1513)

Breaking Open the Story

Not being able to conceive a child was a deep disappointment and
a source of suffering for this couple. It led them to ask difficult
questions of God and of themselves.

+ Recall one of your recent disappointments in family life.
  What questions do you remember asking God and yourself
  in that situation?
+ Amid this couple's shared pain, questioning, and disappointment, positive consequences began to emerge in their life
  together. In the disappointments you recalled, are you aware
  of any positive gains, any new skills learned or benefits received?
+ This couple's questioning and prayer continued, but began
  to change in a significant way. In what ways did your prayer
  and searching change as time unfolded?

More Than Meets the Eye

How can we begin to discover new life present within the disappointments and sufferings of family living? In watching their story
unfold, this couple is transformed through a crisis of infertility to a
new way of giving life. We see that it is a journey in three movements: facing their infertility, accepting and embracing it, and being
transformed through it. These three movements are the journey of
Christian life as exemplified by Jesus Christ.

Facing the Suffering

The Irish Catholic upbringing of this storyteller did not prepare her for infertility, and her infertility raised religious questions: "Why is God punishing us?" and "Why would God allow those who didn't want children to become pregnant?" When things did not go the way she assumed they would or should, this crisis prompted her to talk about God and to God.

God expects us to ask for what we want or need. Initially, as we face our sufferings, our asking may slip into an attitude of control, seeking to convince God of our own personal plan . . . a prayer that could become, "God, I know what's good, right, and holy in this situation; now you'd better hurry up and bring it about."

Embracing the Suffering

When we begin to embrace what is, a shift happens in the way we pray and live. The wrestling match in our prayer, between God's way and ours, changes to become a more open trust of God's mysterious plan. What becomes dominant is the posture of Jesus. For instance, in the garden the night before the Crucifixion, Jesus told the Father his desire, "Remove this cup from me." Then, without so much as a pause for breath, he continued, "Yet, not my will but yours be done" (Luke 22:42). His prayer certainly asks, but then draws him to trust God's will, even if God's will is the exact opposite of what he desires.

The couple's prayer of asking made it possible to let go of their own agenda or control and embrace God's will. Their act of begging God for a child changed both them and their petitions, "Our prayer turned to a more inclusive vision of parenthood."

Transformed Through the Suffering

This movement of their hearts toward God's will was not simply the decision of the couple, it was the work of the spirit of God within them. They were being transformed. This couple became "fertile," in other words, life-giving, in ways they might not have expected. They found themselves more sensitive to others' trials, strengthened in teaching other people's children, and open to adoption. In effect this couple's infertility became the arena for God to transmit and serve life in ways they never anticipated.

Families are called to trust that God will use everything, even the sufferings and confusions of life, to transform them. Slowly we are opened to the gifts God is offering.

Praying

For this ritual time, you will need at least ten to fifteen minutes, a calm setting, and a reflective spirit, one that is willing to enter into a Scripture story as it unfolds.

1. Prepare yourself for prayer by taking two minutes to relax your body and release your mind.

2. Read slowly and thoughtfully these words taken from Jeremiah. Try to enter the story fully.

> The word that came to Jeremiah from the LORD: "Come, go down to the potter's house, and there I will let you hear my words." So I went down to the potter's house, and there he was working at his wheel. The vessel he was making of clay was spoiled in the potter's hand, and he reworked it into another vessel, as seemed good to him.
>
> Then the word of the LORD came to me: Can I not do with you, O house of Israel, just as this potter has done? says the LORD. Just like the clay in the potter's hand, so are you in my hand, O house of Israel.
>
> (Jeremiah 18:1–6)

3. Reflect for a few moments on these questions:
- What in my life seems to be "spoiled"?
- How is God reworking my clay into something new?

4. Pray today, tomorrow, and for many days in the future, these words of Psalm 139:1–6:

> O LORD, you have searched me and known me.
> You know when I sit down and when I rise up;
>   you discern my thoughts from far away.

You search out my path and my lying down,
    and are acquainted with all my ways.
Even before a word is on my tongue,
    O LORD, you know it completely.
You hem me in, behind and before,
    and lay your hand upon me.
Such knowledge is too wonderful for me;
    it is so high that I cannot attain it.

Before leading a group through this ritual, be sure to have Bibles for all members. In preparation for this prayer, have supplies ready so that each person may create a bookmark listing the two Scripture passages. Then with Bibles and bookmarks in hand, lead the prayer.

After the prayer is finished, encourage all to take their bookmarks home, to again sit with these Scripture texts as each may need to or be called to.

THE STORY TOLD A Family Embrace

Last Christmas my thirty-two-year-old brother, Bob, who lives in another state, came home and announced to us that he had been in an Alcoholics Anonymous program for one month. He knew the trip home would be difficult as he faced family and friends with this information. Few of us had known the extent to which alcoholism had invaded his life, career, and relationships. Our family listened, cried, hugged, and loved him, hoping he could add all of that to his fragile support system when he headed back to Minnesota.

Two months later his longtime woman friend and companion broke off their relationship. She had been his best friend and strongest supporter for three years. The devastation of the breakup, along with a draining bout of the flu, was almost enough to break his spirit as well as his alcohol abstinence.

During that time one of our sisters called him and heard the whole story. She read between the lines and knew that he needed his family. She called the rest of us (there are eight children in our family), and we all decided we had to figure out a way to go to him. We wanted to bring our energy and strength to him not only as a symbol of our solidarity with him but also to show our deep love and concern.

After hundreds of phone calls and numerous arrangements for our families and jobs, we piled into a van and headed north. The weekend was filled with laughter, spontaneity, silliness, long talks, and oceans of love. He told us later that our presence fed and nourished his fragile spirit for weeks. We had given him some gifts for his apartment when we left, but he said that the gift he will always treasure is our presence to him that weekend. In return he fed all of us by allowing us to love and nurture him, and by being open to us. He did survive that traumatic time in his life, and as I write this story, he is about to celebrate his first year of sobriety.

Mysteriously, what looks like loss, failure, or death on the outside is later seen as growth, gift, new life. Paradoxically, our "dyings" are often the impetus for new insights, new skills, new life.

(Adapted from Joseph A. Torma, *First Church,* pp. 7–8)

Breaking Open the Story

In order to cope with his alcoholism, Bob realized he needed more help, so he risked sharing his secret with a family member.

♦ Recall a time when you revealed a difficult truth about yourself to others?

When Bob was able to share his secret, his brothers and sisters walked through that new door in ways that surprised him, and that proved to be exactly what he needed.

♦ How have others surprised you by their unanticipated goodness in response to your need?

More Than Meets the Eye

Bob was faced with two deeply significant issues: his alcoholism and the end of a long-term relationship. In addition to coping with the difficulties of such problems, Bob may have experienced feelings of failure or worthlessness, feelings of being unloved and unlovable. Often feelings like these may tempt all of us to close ourselves off, separating, even isolating, ourselves.

Bob took a chance, telling his "whole story" to one of his sisters. The result was an overwhelming opportunity for faithful love to flow within his family. The treasured gift of their presence on that weekend was able to sustain "his fragile spirit for weeks." Genuine love is found and expressed in the connections within family, bonds that do not break just because problems arise.

Bob's experience of family presence and solidarity can be seen as communion in its deepest sense: diverse parts united as one for the benefit of one another. Remember the words of Saint Paul, "To each is given the manifestation of the Spirit for the common good" (1 Corinthians 12:7). Bob's sisters and brothers rearranged their work schedules, found baby-sitters, rented a van, and so on, for the common good: support of Bob. Through these simple acts, they united themselves with one another and with Bob in communion. Such family food, substantial though invisible, nourished all with a tangible something that each was able to live on!

When families do this, even in simple ways, they stand on holy ground. No one ever journeys alone. Christ walks with us, but so often his face looks like that of our own sisters. Christ feeds us with life and the strength to carry on faithfully through hands that appear to be those of our brothers. On our pilgrim way, the presence of Christ is often revealed in our own family.

Praying

Find a fairly large, empty bowl, such as a mixing bowl from your kitchen or a decorative pottery or ceramic bowl from a display. Bring it to your prayer space.

1. Sit comfortably with the bowl resting in your lap, cupping it with your hands. Close your eyes and breathe a few deep, cleansing breaths.

2. Imagine various family members who at this moment "hunger," not physically but emotionally, psychologically, spiritually.

3. Focus on one particular family member, perhaps the one who is most in need today. Try to define the hunger in her or his life.

4. Pray this mantra several times over:

Lord,
grant me a compassionate heart,
an open mind,
and an imaginative spirit . . .
all to respond lovingly to his or her hunger.

5. Lift the bowl from your lap, feeling its weight, its shape, its details. As you do this, and with your eyes still closed, do the following:

- Recall ways you are already feeding this person's hunger, filling his or her bowl.

- Consider how you might feed this loved one all the more in the immediate future, diminishing her or his emptiness.

6. Choose one of the options for "feeding" your relative. Resolve to act.

7. Stand, and return the bowl to its shelf. As you do so, pray: "Amen, Lord, amen! Let it be so."

If this ritual is to be prayed with a group, make arrangements to have enough soup or salad bowls for all members to use. Follow the ritual instructions as given, until step 7. Adapt the final gesture in this way: "Stand with your bowl in hand, and individually come forward, gently placing your bowl on our prayer table. As you do so, pray aloud: 'Amen, Lord, amen! Let it be so.'" A procession of participants should slowly take place, until all bowls have been reverently placed on the prayer table. Some quiet background music may be played during this ritual gesture and procession.

THE STORY TOLD Aunt Clare

M y aunt Clare was in her eighties when she had a disabling stroke. A few of my adult children went to the hospital with me to visit her for the first time. She couldn't speak; only a guttural sound came out when she tried. Her face was lopsided and her hair in wild disarray.

This dear woman was always perfectly groomed and intelligent, a career woman who was never able to have children. Because of not having children of her own, she doted on her nieces and nephews. In Aunt Clare's eyes, we could do no wrong; she loved us no matter what. She was the strong, stable, kind, and compassionate confidant. And now she could only reach out with one arm, desperately trying to say something.

I was totally shattered to see her in such a pitiable state, and became immobilized by my grief. Without hesitation my son Dave reached across the bed, gathered her to his chest, and rocked her back and forth. I could see the fear leave her eyes, and a feeling of peace was almost tangible. The scene is etched forever in my heart.

> There is a Job-like mystery in human suffering and loss that can't be comprehended with reason. It can only be lived in faith. Suffering forces our attention toward places we would normally neglect.
>
> (Thomas Moore, *Care of the Soul*, p. 258)

Breaking Open the Story

We see two responses to Aunt Clare's illness; both reactions are common enough. The first is that of the storyteller: "I was totally shattered . . . and became immobilized by my grief."

♦ Describe what it is that immobilizes you at such times.

The second response is that of Dave, who said nothing yet was able to offer a tremendous embrace, gathering Aunt Clare to his chest and rocking her.

♦ What do embraces or other physical expressions of care communicate to you in moments such as this?

More Than Meets the Eye

It is shattering to encounter someone so beloved suffering a severe illness. In addition to losing her health, Aunt Clare was in danger of losing her sense of dignity. The mere presence of her family affirmed in her that she is worthwhile and of great value, not for what she can provide or do, but simply in and of herself. An important dimension of family is its care and service of human life from cradle to grave. With this family, serving life happened through the experience of being present to Aunt Clare at a difficult time in her life.

In times of illness, the church offers a comforting ritual in the sacrament of Anointing. In the first part of the Rite of Anointing, the Scriptures are read. God's word reminds us of our history, our identity, of the fact that we are never alone in our struggles. Then the anointing with oil takes place; symbolically and physically, oil can soothe open wounds, aches, and pains.

The use of oil and caring touch are comforting gestures. We may even see this family's action toward Aunt Clare as a kind of anointing. The gathering of her clan reminds her of who she is, her history, her value. This family's presence speaks loudly that she does not walk alone in her suffering, and will not walk alone toward her eventual death. Dave's embrace becomes like an oil of anointing, surrounding her wounds and binding them up. That embrace is the oil that removes her fear and quiets her troubled spirit. His gathering her to his chest and rocking back and forth is a real sacred moment, wherein God's presence and peace is almost tangible.

There is a special kind of touch that only family can provide. They anoint in ordinary ways, with hugs, embraces, and memories. These acts of affection heal the soul.

Praying

Before sitting down, pour a small amount of oil in an easily accessible container. Bring this and some type of towel to your place of prayer. (Olive oil, cooking oil, or any body lotion could be used.)

1. Sit comfortably in your chair, breathing deeply and slowly for several minutes. Close your eyes and listen to the sound of your breathing, your own heart beating.

2. Open your eyes again and dip the fingertips of one of your hands into the oil. Rub your fingertips together, feeling the smoothness of the oil.

3. Close your eyes and begin an anointing ritual by tracing the sign of the cross several times on your other hand or your forehead.

4. As you do this, recall an embrace, a touch, a comforting pat on the back from another person that brought you peace or encouragement when you needed it. If no memory surfaces, imagine the touch of Jesus now as you sit quietly. Savor this experience for a few moments.

5. End your prayer time with a self-composed prayer of thanksgiving for this particular person (or for all people), who has anointed you with an act of affection, one that has fed your soul.

If this ritual is to be prayed in a group setting, provide oil in a container that can be passed easily from one person to the next, perhaps in a small bowl. Sit in a circle, near enough to one another to facilitate this sharing of the oil. Be sure to have enough paper towels, napkins, or cloth towels for people to wipe away any excess oil.

THE STORY TOLD Touching!

For our twenty-fifth wedding anniversary, my wife gave me a picture album with photos of the two of us from the time we started dating up to the present.

As I paged through the years, I was struck with the way we touched each other in all those pictures: holding hands in front of a fountain, arm in arm on the beach, sitting on my lap at a picnic table, sitting on the sofa with her head on my shoulder. I thought about how connected we are by our touching each other over these twenty-five years, and what a great gift that is in our marriage, and in my life.

I recall holding her hand as she was rolled down the hallway to surgery recently, and the reassurance of our daily kisses good-bye in the morning. I think of how calming it is when she rubs the back of my shoulders after a tense day at work.

Our touching each other, even when it's done unconsciously, connects us on a level we seldom talk about. Touch seems to strengthen our life together whether we are making love or just holding hands during the sad part of a movie. It seems that something passes between us, a kind of energy that is sometimes passion, sometimes reassurance or comfort or peace.

Some of the ways we touch are so much a part of our daily routine that we are not even aware of their effect on us; her taking my arm when she wears high-heeled shoes or our "sleeping like spoons" on cold winter nights.

I grew up in a family where we hardly ever touched one another except when it was necessary. Maybe that's why I was so struck by the effect touch has had on our life together.

We received a lot of gifts on our twenty-fifth anniversary, but that album is my favorite!

Touching grasps, stimulates, changes our bodies. Words, too, can have something of the same effect. But they can also resound ineffectively. One cannot miss a touch. The body notices being touched.

> What makes the skin unique as compared with all other organs is that it is turned both outwards and inwards, so that it can communicate what is happening within us outwards and outside experiences inwards.
>
> (Elisabeth Moltmann-Wendel, *I Am My Body*, p. 60)

Breaking Open the Story

This husband steps back from his twenty-five years of marriage to recognize how deeply he appreciates being physically close to his wife. Simple gestures of touching are especially important to this man whose family did not express affection in this way.

♦ Recall your growing-up years. To what extent was physical touch a means of communicating with one another? How has that affected your comfort level with touch now?

In looking at his album, this husband concludes that ongoing physical contact with his wife has strengthened and energized their marriage.

♦ Name some ways that physical touch affects your intimate relationships with spouse, children, loved ones.

More Than Meets the Eye

This married man was struck by something very ordinary going on in all the pictures of his anniversary album. The experience of being touched by his wife in a variety of ways takes on a deeper meaning as he steps back to notice how consistently touch has filled his life.

The process of stepping back and reflecting on their married life together gave this husband an increased awareness of "something" that passed between them when flesh touches flesh. He refers to this something as "energy," "reassurance," and "comfort." Touch communicates both passion and peace to him. Such simple gestures are powerful experiences that bind two people together and communicate more than words can describe.

Love is communicated through the flesh—whether in deep passion or polite gestures. Christians believe that God communicated divine love through his own flesh in Jesus of Nazareth. This enfleshment of God's love is called the Incarnation. The mystery of the Incarnation, God communicating self through human flesh, did not last just thirty-three years. When Jesus was raised from the dead, he promised to remain with humanity for all time. The risen Christ dwells among us *in the flesh* of those who follow him.

This truth gives married couples the privilege of communicating God's love to one another on a day-to-day basis through the simple gift of touching one another. In these ordinary human interactions of touch, God continues to create and give life.

Praying

1. Sit quietly with your hands relaxed in your lap.

2. Take a long and careful look at your hands. Notice their size and shape; see any lines, scratches, and wear; flex your fingers and feel the strength.

3. Call to mind all the people your hands have touched just in the past twenty-four hours.

4. As you consider these people, reflect on the different ways your hands were used, both for good and for ill.

5. Does any one experience of touch (whether good or ill) stand out in your mind? If so, try to relive the entire situation, from the moment the two of you came together through the time of your parting.
   - If your hand remembrance was good, offer a prayer of thanksgiving for hands used well, hands used as Jesus would use them.
   - If your hand remembrance was not good, offer a prayer of petition to God for patience, fortitude, self-confidence, humility, and so on—whatever the situation may have called for but did not receive through your hands.

6. End your prayer by making a resolution to use your hands intentionally for the good of others in days to come. After all, hands

are capable of communicating the love, compassion, forgiveness, and healing of Jesus to those you touch.

As a reminder to yourself, if you regularly wear a ring, why not switch it to the other hand for a few days. Each time you see or feel it there, recall your resolution to touch others well.

When used with a group, this prayer ritual might be most effective if the leader asks the participants to share the "experience of touch" that surfaced within them during the quiet reflection of step 5. This sharing should take place with only one person, because some experiences may be rather personal. After a sufficient time has passed, the leader should invite the group to make their closing resolutions privately. When this silent period is finished, the leader should stand before the group, and while switching her or his ring from one hand to the other, explain the rationale of this gesture.

THE STORY TOLD When Truth Hurts

My husband, Bill, had been ill for a long time. He had a brain tumor. When he was finally hospitalized, my young son said very little at the time. Then suddenly one morning he asked, "Mummy, is my daddy going to die?" I wanted desperately to deny it, but simply answered, "Yes, darling, he is." Anthony kept munching his cereal, trying not to cry, and then quietly he crept onto my lap and sobbed and sobbed. He sat there for a long time. And as I cradled my son, I wished with all my heart that I could shield him from this pain. But I knew that I could not, nor did I have the right to do so. This was his experience. I could not bear it for him. I was there to support him, not to take away his pain.

> Let me not pray to be sheltered from dangers but to be fearless in facing them.
> Let me not beg for the stilling of my pain but for the heart to conquer it.
> (Rabindranath Tagore, "Fruit-Gathering," as quoted in *On Death and Dying*, by Elisabeth Kübler-Ross, MD, p. 1)

Breaking Open the Story

For a few moments, identify with Anthony's mother. This mother "wished with all my heart that I could shield him from this pain," but she realized Bill's immanent death was an experience that was rightfully Anthony's. She had the courage not only to face the truth but also to speak the truth.

- Describe a time when you had the responsibility to tell a difficult truth to another. In what ways did you consider the other while you shared this news?
- Now identify with Anthony. Recall a situation in which a difficult truth was told to you. How might someone tell you the truth so that you could best receive it?

More Than Meets the Eye

This wife and mother had the courage to speak the truth to her son. She chose to nurture life in the midst of death. She herself must have already faced and accepted (at least to some degree) the fact of Bill's immanent death. At first glance, denying the truth of Bill's impending death may appear to spare Anthony from pain. However, it would only frustrate his grieving process. Mom's simple truth-sharing allowed genuine grief to surface now in her son. She recognized that for her son to have fullness of life, he had to embrace death, even at this tender age.

Anthony had a right to know how serious his father's condition was, and she told him clearly and in a proper proportion that he could understand. Truth-telling requires sensitivity to the truth-hearer. Just as this mother would serve appropriate kinds and amounts of food to Anthony, so too did she serve up truth about life (and death) in proper proportions that he could digest.

This mother also showed great wisdom by giving her son the time and space to choose his own way of dealing with this devastating news. She did not impose her experience of loss onto him, but allowed him to sit quietly, creep into her lap, then sob. Anthony was able to do what he felt was necessary.

Mom also spoke the truth within a context of comfort and support. She cradled her son, not taking his pain away but assuring him that he was not alone in that pain. A healthy family provides such a safe, secure environment in which painful truth can be shared. Like Simon carrying the cross of Jesus (Matthew 27:32), a family can help carry heavy burdens—not by taking them away but by providing enough support so the weight of such crosses does not crush.

Such valuing of her son's pain shows a reverence for life as it really is. This helps to create an atmosphere wherein God can be noticed and called on. God does tend lovingly to all our wounds; the Divine Physician heals all brokenness and grieving hearts, choosing to do so through the love and care of family members, even in their most difficult moments. Undoubtedly this is holy.

Praying

For this prayer time, you will need a weight or a heavy rock, something that will cause you to strain a bit as you hold it for a few moments.

1. Begin by standing with the rock or weight in your hands. Close your eyes, and for a few moments, feel its heaviness, feel your own muscles pulling, accept the weight being in your hands.

2. Be seated, placing the rock or weight in your lap, but still touching it with your hands. While doing so, try to relate its heaviness to a difficult truth someone has shared with you recently.

3. Imagine yourself embracing this difficult truth, this burden of another. Imagine the weight in your lap being halved, as now two people carry it.

4. Now ask God for two graces:

- not to deny but to accept this difficult truth
- willingness to be present to and journey with this person

5. Pray Psalm 23 slowly, reflectively:

The LORD is my shepherd, I shall not want.
    He makes me lie down in green pastures;
he leads me beside still waters;
    he restores my soul.
He leads me in right paths
    for his name's sake.

Even though I walk through the darkest valley,
    I fear no evil;
for you are with me;
        your rod and your staff—
        they comfort me.

You prepare a table before me
        in the presence of my enemies;
you anoint my head with oil;
        my cup overflows.

> Surely goodness and mercy shall follow me
>> all the days of my life,
> and I shall dwell in the house of the LORD
>> my whole life long.

6. Bend over, releasing the rock or weight onto the floor. Acknowledge the shepherding care of the risen Lord, who is already carrying this heavy burden. Carry this image of the Good Shepherd (do not carry the burden) with you throughout the day.

If this ritual is to be done with a group, arrange for a box of rocks, a stack of books, or a sufficient number of heavy objects to be on hand. Pass these out to all participants before beginning. The prayer may then follow the outline as given.

THE STORY TOLD The Housekeeping Blues

One more load of laundry . . . how, I asked myself, could five people produce that many shorts and shirts? (And where were the mates to the last dozen assorted socks at the bottom of the basket?) It's a job I detest because it's never done. Next to grocery shopping, it's the least rewarding job I do, like filling a pitcher with a hole in the bottom.

The children help with chores, but my job is a never-ending process of doing, or supervising the doing, of monotonous details, such as making sure notebook paper is in the cupboard for school assignments, calling the repair person to fix the washer, and holding kids accountable for their fair share of house and yard work.

It's not just the monotony but the seeming insignificance of many things I do daily. I much prefer reading a story or taking the children to visit their uncle Dick. Then I feel I'm doing something really important, being with my family. Something about housekeeping is lonely, or boring at best. I find myself complaining about how much there is to do and how little time there is to do it. I often feel that much of the work of housekeeping is not appreciated, or even noticed, except when it doesn't get done (like "Where's the toilet paper?" when we are completely out).

For the first few years of parenting, I actually found rewarding the everyday duties of changing diapers, making doctor's appointments, paying the paperboy, and endless carpools. There was the sense of being the organizer, or maybe the conductor of a "symphony of living," bringing all the elements of my family into harmony. Those were my more idealistic days. Now I come home from work, divide up the tasks, and do what I can because somebody has to do it. I wouldn't call it noble or anything, just necessary.

Without love even those deeds that earn prestige, wealth, and power become hollow and empty. With love, the smallest, most ordinary of actions becomes sacred.

67

(Ernest Boyer Jr., *Finding God at Home*, p. 92)

Breaking Open the Story

This mother "sings the blues" of doing endless chores for her family, and describes how she views household tasks.

♦ What feelings welled up in your recollections of housekeeping chores? Can you identify with her blues?

When this mother considers how she deals with the thousand thankless tasks of daily family living, she seems resigned when she says, "Now I come home from work, divide up the tasks, and do what I can because somebody has to do it."

♦ Are mundane family chores really endurance tests? Is there actually a purpose to them?

♦ What do you believe about home or family that motivates you to invest your time and energy in these tasks?

More Than Meets the Eye

This mother, in the throes of the "blues," does not seem to find God in her household chores. Usually families associate the presence of God with "churchy" moments, such as baptisms, weddings, first Communions, funerals, Sunday Eucharist, the family rosary, or prayer time together. Certainly these events are very important moments of contact with God. However, family members are also challenged to discover God at work right where they live: in bathrooms, carpools, and laundry. "Family spirituality is rooted in the earth . . . in the hard labors of our hands" (Wendy M. Wright, *Sacred Dwelling*, p. 194).

Sometimes we get fooled by the magnitude (or lack thereof) of particular tasks. We erroneously believe that the more grandiose the accomplishment, the more value it must have, and the more sacred it could be. Conversely, meager tasks (busywork) can be seen as meaningless, even unholy. This housekeeper complains that "it's not just the monotony but the seeming insignificance of many things I do daily." In doing what is necessary, this storyteller is invited to die to self in a sense, in order to be faithful to the promise made when she said yes to marriage. That promise of fidelity, made by both spouses, is at the heart of family. One essential part of faithfulness is to serve life, which at its basic level means clothing, feeding, and cleaning.

"Truly I tell you, just as you did it to one of the least of these who are members of my family, you did it to me" (Matthew 25:40). In this Gospel passage, Jesus is telling us clearly that large or small, mundane or lofty tasks done in service of one another are sacred. This housekeeper is not just serving her family, she is serving Christ. Recognizing this can make housekeeping chores no longer merely necessary but truly noble acts. God is encountered in the service of others, and revealed in remaining faithful to promises made.

Praying

1. "Sanctify the moment" (as the following prayer reminds you) by calming down, breathing deeply and rhythmically for a few moments to relax.

2. Pray these words to our God:

O Common One,
you are so plain,
so familiar, so simple
that we miss you in our desire for some other novelty. We seek
you in mystery, ritual, knowledge, magic—all the things we hope
will take away our pain and imperfection. We think that if we can
just become enlightened, then we will be one with you.

> And here you are, brokenhearted,
> loving us so much, hurrying toward us,
> risking everything to be with us in our unenlightenment.

Jesus, you are *things as they are.*
Here is where I meet you in such quiet splendor and beauty and
completion. Over and over as I bump up against imperfection,
resistance, fear—there you are, grinning at me,

sanctifying the moment redeeming redeeming redeeming in
streaming satin rivers
of Grace   what is so.

(From *making Haggodesh*, July 1991)

3. Carry back to your day a renewed confidence that God is
indeed "sanctifying the moment . . . redeeming redeeming redeeming" you!

Because this prayer addresses God as "O Common One," if a
group is celebrating this ritual, make sure that each participant has
a personal copy of the prayer. After quieting down, one person
should invite the group to recite "in common" all these words and
phrases.

THE STORY TOLD No Such Thing As Perfect!

When our daughter told us she was sexually involved with her boyfriend and that they were living together, we were very hurt and disappointed. Phil and I cried for about a week. We told her how we felt about her decision and shared our strong belief that sex is part of marriage. We launched a letter-writing campaign trying desperately to change her mind. After a while, when nothing changed her mind, we were angry.

We questioned our parenting. We blamed her boyfriend. We were embarrassed to tell our friends and hurt by her rejection of our values. But we didn't want to come down on her too hard for fear she might think we were rejecting her completely, so we sprinkled love and encouragement in our letters. We kept telling ourselves that we raised our children to be independent thinkers and that we could not make our children's decisions for them for the rest of their lives. We felt we knew what was best for them, but they had made their own decisions and there was nothing we could do to change their minds.

> Hope is a state of mind, not of the world. Hope, in this deep and powerful sense, is not the same as joy that things are going well, or willingness to invest in enterprises that are obviously heading for success, but rather an ability to work for something because it is good.
>
> (Vaclav Havel)

Breaking Open the Story

The pain in this story is an all-too-common one for parents: feelings of disappointment and failure when raising children.

♦ When have you ever asked yourself, "Where did I go wrong as a parent"?

Notice how these folks were sensitive in their method of correction: "We didn't want to come down on her too hard for fear she might think we were rejecting her completely, so we sprinkled love and encouragement in our letters."

♦ Reflect on the way you confront family members. To what extent are you able to criticize an action while continuing to love the person?

More Than Meets the Eye

This couple struggles with their daughter's choice of society's values rather than those of the Gospel. Her choosing premarital sex rather than chastity leaves them hurt, disappointed, even angry. Parenting is not an easy task. No doubt every parent has had some experiences of failure and self-doubt when trying to teach and positively influence their children. At such times the basic reasoning of parents so often follows these lines: Because our child chose to live differently from what we taught, desired, and hoped for, we must have done something wrong!

In contrast to this kind of "logic," consider the image of God parenting the first man and woman in the garden, as told in the opening chapters of Genesis. God gave them everything: their physical needs of food and shelter; companionship, for they were a couple (not to mention their quite personal relationship with God); even rewarding work ("masters" of all creation). Yet recall what they did. They disobeyed, choosing to act on their own. God "understands" what it feels like to have children who opt to live in opposition to the divine plan.

Continuing with this image from Genesis, God reveals various qualities of holy parenting:

- total acceptance of us, with all our limitations
- patience with our slowness to respond
- forgiveness of our failures
- perseverance in bringing us back

The holiness of our parenting lies in seeking to imitate these qualities of God's unconditional love, not in producing children who act perfectly.

Just as raising perfect children is an impossibility for us, so too loving unconditionally is a task at which we will undoubtedly fall short. This couple is challenged to live out their faith in God by seeking to love their daughter, even to forgive her, while still giving witness to their own Gospel values.

Praying

Make sure you have at least ten to fifteen minutes of undisturbed, quiet time.

1. Sit comfortably, and with your eyes closed, breathe deeply several times, noticing the air move in and out, feeling your chest rise and fall.

2. Pray slowly, thoughtfully, reflectively (and repeatedly, if helpful) this prayer called "Letting Go." If so drawn, pause and repeat one line or phrase, allowing it to sink deeply into your being.

To a dear one about whom I have been concerned.
I behold the Christ in you.
I place you lovingly in the care of the Father.
I release you from my anxiety and concern.
I let go of my possessive hold on you.
I am willing to free you to follow the dictates of your indwelling Lord.
I am willing to free you to live your life according to your best light and understanding.
Husband, wife, child, friend—
I no longer try to force my ideas on you, my ways on you.
I lift my thoughts above you, above the personal level.
I see you as God sees you, a spiritual being, created in His image, and endowed with qualities and abilities that make you needed, and important—not only to me but to God and His larger plan.
I do not bind you, I no longer believe that you do not have the understanding you need in order to meet life.

I bless you,
I have faith in you,
I behold Jesus in you.
(Author unknown, as quoted in *Freedom*,
by Jacqueline Syrup Bergan and S. Marie Schwan, p. 143)

3. Carry with you the comfort of this prayer as you move through your day. Your "husband, wife, child, friend" has been placed securely in the hands of God.

When this prayer is to be shared in a group setting, be sure to make enough copies of "Letting Go" so that each participant may have her or his own copy. On completing the common prayer, ask the members to share with one another anything they felt or thought as they prayed "Letting Go." Sometimes the insight of another may elicit even more wisdom within the self.

THE STORIES TOLD Growing Up

We were all in the family room—the kids playing, Ken reading, and I working on the computer. Paul was sitting on the floor amid his toys, half chewing on them, half playing with them as ten-month-olds do.

Suddenly he hoisted himself up on the sofa, turned toward the fireplace, and walked across the room to the hearth, stood there for a second, then sat down with a huge smile and began to clap his hands with glee. He looked to be very pleased with himself. We all joined in clapping with him, delighted at his newfound independence. He seemed so full of himself, so unconsciously proud that he had done something wonderful . . . and he was loving it!

Allison's first comment was, "Wow, what a feeling of power." She had been behind the wheel of the car for only five minutes, tracing the lines of the huge school parking lot where I had taken her for her first lesson.

Backing the car out of the garage without denting or scraping anything was her first accomplishment. She heaved an audible sigh of relief at the bottom of the driveway. The first turn was a surprise to her. It was harder than it looked, she said, getting the wheel back to straight without sending passengers flying against the door.

She was full of questions: "What if the light turns when you're just about at the corner? Who has the right of way in a parking lot?" Suddenly she was very quiet, concentrating on every move, savoring the feeling of speeding up and slowing down at will.

Then another string of questions: "How long before she could drive with her friends in the car? What would they think when they saw her behind the wheel? How would she pay for gas?" I tried to answer as best I could, all the while encouraging her to concentrate on what she was doing at the moment.

It seems that she was doing more than having her first driving lesson. It was like she wanted to know and be able to do everything all at once, yesterday! And all I could think about was how grown up she looked for a fifteen-year-old, and how dangerous it was on the streets for inexperienced drivers . . . and how much the insurance would cost. I had this feeling that although we were both in the same car at the same time, we were really in entirely different places.

> The difficult task of parenthood is to help children grow to the freedom that permits them to stand on their own feet, physically, mentally and spiritually, and to allow them to move away in their own direction.
>
> (Henri J. M. Nouwen, *Reaching Out*, p. 83)

Breaking Open the Stories

Paul's first steps were moments of delight; likewise Allison was filled with questions and wonder as she learned to drive.

- ♦ What kind of feelings or questions do you associate with times of transition in your life?

Take a moment to examine the parents in these stories; they too are changing as their children learn new skills. Their role is more than that of mere observers; each parent actually participates in her or his child's transition.

- ♦ Like these parents, when have you walked with someone in a transition? In what ways did your participation affect you? affect the one in transition?

More Than Meets the Eye

When parents see a crawling child stand up and walk, or an unsure teenager gain the confidence to drive, they are witnessing a power beyond their control. Michelangelo, the great Italian artist, recognized and gave due credit to this power. When praised for the quality of his sculptures, he replied that the figures were already in the stone; all he did was allow them to emerge! Likewise neither the child nor the parent is the source of growth in these transitions; all they can do is assist it, guide it, and allow it to emerge. This power is none other than the creative hand of God. When parents affirm a child's first step and answer questions to dispel fears, they are cooperating with the divine Creator in the growth of their child.

Such transitions of growth are also times of vulnerability for both child and parent alike. Whenever new skills are being learned, are still unmastered, accidents can happen! Children fall, fender benders occur, injuries can result. Although parents may see the pitfalls and even feel anxious about them, they need to balance their appropriate caution with a recognition of their child's ability and the guiding care of God. They realize they are not in control of the changes taking place. It is better to work and move with the creative hand of God, in a posture of trust.

A scriptural image may clarify this relationship. God states, "Just like the clay in the potter's hand, so are you in my hand, O house of Israel" (Jeremiah 18:6). A child (the clay) is formed by both God's design and parental shaping. The power of God guides parents in cooperating with the growth of their children. Often a parent's response at this time will be that of awe, pure and simple!

Predictable times of change and growth, such as driving lessons and first steps, are holy, for God is the source of them all. Parents serve life well when they simply assist and cooperate with these inner workings of God's own hand.

Praying

We seek to step back in awe as we contemplate the growth in someone close to us, always in God's time, not our own.

1. Sit quietly with your eyes closed. Focus all your attention inward, noticing your heart beating. Feel its rhythm, and let its regularity calm your inner being.

2. In your imagination, picture a loved one who is currently in a period of transition, changing some aspect of his or her life. Describe the transition as clearly as you can, for example, how long it has been happening, what is already in place, and so on.

3. Read and reflect on these words from the author of Ecclesiastes:

> For everything there is a season, and a time for every matter under heaven:
>> a time to be born, and a time to die;
>> a time to plant, and a time to pluck up what is planted;
>> a time to kill, and a time to heal;
>> a time to break down, and a time to build up;
>> a time to weep, and a time to laugh;
>> a time to mourn, and a time to dance;
>> a time to throw away stones, and a time to gather stones
>>> together;
>> a time to embrace, and a time to refrain from embracing;
>> a time to seek, and a time to lose;
>> a time to keep, and a time to throw away;
>> a time to tear, and a time to sew;
>> a time to keep silence, and a time to speak;
>> a time to love, and a time to hate;
>> a time for war, and a time for peace.
>
> What gain have the workers from their toil? I have seen the business that God has given to everyone to be busy with. He has made everything suitable for its time.
>
> (3:1–11)

Now question yourself:

- What has been my posture or role in relation to this loved one as she or he has undergone change?
- What role or posture might I take now?

4. Create your own two-sentence prayer of supplication. Ask for a deeper trust of God, for it is God who brings about transformation, always in God's own time.

When sharing this prayer as a group, ask the participants to share aloud (if each feels comfortable doing so) their prayers of supplication from step 4. When all have spoken, the leader may close with the words: "Loving God, who never turns a deaf ear to our cries, listen to and answer us in your time, for we seek your way, and your way alone. We ask this of you through Christ our Lord. Amen."

Developing Society

A family's responsibility moves beyond caring for itself into the extended family, the neighborhood, the city, and the world. When parents teach children to take turns, to share what they have with others, to respect other persons and their property, to understand rules and accept the consequences of breaking them, and to practice hospitality, they are preparing their children for good citizenship as well as building up society itself.

Setting such standards for behavior may not seem holy to most parents or children, but how persons treat one another has always been central in the Judeo-Christian tradition. Jesus commands his disciples to "love the Lord your God with all your whole heart, and with all your soul, and with all your mind, [and] . . . your neighbor as yourself" (Matthew 22:37–39). Faith-filled families bring to the larger society their experience of placing the common good above individual wants, and of valuing persons over things. When families lose sight of these values, society surely does too.

Thus the family has the dual task of forming committed disciples for the Kingdom and good citizens for this world.

THE STORY TOLD Broken Windows

I returned home from the grocery store to the scene of the crime: a half dozen eleven- and twelve-year-old boys, a makeshift baseball diamond, and the neighbor's broken window. When I walked into the backyard, I knew right away something was wrong.

Gradually the story began to emerge—in four or five versions. The excuses came first: the sun was in the batter's eyes, and the guy in right field tripped and missed the fly ball that hit the window. No one named the batter; it was an accident!

I was angry. They had been told many times not to play ball in the backyard, but to use the empty lot several blocks away. After they brought the groceries in and I had let off some steam, I tried to get the two more talkative boys to reveal what had actually happened. They agreed that Josh was at bat when it happened and that he should pay for the window. Josh argued that he had wanted to play at the lot several blocks away, and that it was Ken's and Skip's idea to play in the yard, so they should go tell the neighbors about the accident. After all the blaming and finger pointing died down, I suggested that Josh write the note explaining what had happened, but that they all pitch in for the window.

Josh was upset; he knew his share of the money would have to be earned doing extra chores or delivering papers. He complained loudly that it wasn't his fault and that he was embarrassed to face the neighbor. He knew that he and his brother were in deeper trouble with us because they allowed the game in our yard, which was definitely forbidden.

With some prodding he wrote the note and put it in the neighbor's front door. After dinner that night, we sat down and explained that there would be some consequences for both of them because they knew the rules and had broken them. We started by saying that they could not play baseball for two weeks. We invited them to make suggestions, and they offered instead to give several hours of help to the neighbor, making up for the inconvenience of replacing the window. In addition they would help clean up the mess.

We agreed with their solution. That night when the neighbor called, I gave the phone to the boys; they both apologized for the mess and said they would pay for the repair. Josh went over that night to help clean up, and arranged for the two of them to clean the neighbor's patio furniture and weed the garden.

It took some prodding to get all the money collected and to get the boys over to the neighbor's on Saturday. But I think they learned a lot in the process. There hasn't been another game in the backyard since then.

> The family is the first school of those social virtues which every society needs.
>
> (Pope John Paul II, *Familiaris Consortio*, no. 36)

Breaking Open the Story

Anyone who spends even limited time with children this age certainly can relate to this story!

- ♦ Recall an instance when you happened upon a "scene of the crime."
- ♦ From your example, what lessons were learned from the children's misbehavior?
- ♦ Name some values you wish to instill in your children.

More Than Meets the Eye

The phrase "raising children" brings to mind words like growth, improvement, even elevation to a new height. These various shadings hold true when seeking to raise children in the ways of Christ. To accomplish this, time, creativity, and perseverance are critical. Mom listened to four or five versions of what happened, made suggestions for a solution, and negotiated the consequences. These routine actions help to mold children one step at a time. This "raising" of the boys' behavior to reflect Gospel values is something very holy.

Jesus' message that "you are the light of the world" (Matthew 5:14) demonstrates that the behavior of believers is visible for all to see. Such "light" of good Gospel living must shine through everyday incidents, even those as common as broken windows. When confronted with situations requiring discipline, parents can let their own light shine through the way they handle them. In turn their children are invited to absorb this light, giving witness to what they know and believe through a variety of equally simple actions: writing notes, repairing the window, offering hours of volunteer work. These children's lights may then shine on their peers and neighbors, illuminating them in ways never imagined.

Many parents see themselves as effective, maybe even holy, only when their children perform well: when they get good grades, are successful in athletics, or are popular with other students. Parents may consider "broken window" experiences as moments showing the unholiness of their family. But the reality is this: Some of the most effective times to "raise" children or to share the light of Christ can be when there is misbehavior. Healthy, appropriate discipline can lead to good disciple making.

Praying

This is a walking-stationary-biblical meditation. You will need access to two rooms, one well lit, the other as dark as possible. You will also need a flashlight.

1. Stand in the well-lit room with your eyes closed, and take a moment to calm yourself internally.

2. Open your eyes, turn on your flashlight, and shine it on various objects. Note how difficult it is to see the beam of light in these circumstances.

3. With the flashlight still on, move into the darkened room. Here, notice how effectively the beam of light is able to illuminate various objects.

4. Stop and remember some past situations:

- when you brought the light of Christ into an already good situation
- when you brought the light of Christ into times of difficulty, failure, or brokenness

Where, when, and how is the light of Christ more noticeable? Most important, why is the light of Christ so illuminating?

5. Recall the words of Saint John from his Gospel: "The light shines in the darkness, and the darkness did not overcome it" (1:5).

6. Pray for the grace to be a constant source of light, especially in the dark situations of life. These are the ones in which Christ's light needs to shine most clearly and faithfully.

If this prayer ritual is shared with a group, the leader must plan ahead. He or she should bring a good flashlight, as well as arrange for access to two rooms, one well lit and the other darkened. If two such rooms are not available, the leader should enlist someone to turn off the lights in the one room at the appropriate time. Is there still a way to incorporate bodily movement? By all means do it! To be effective this prayer will take a bit of prior planning.

THE STORY TOLD The Tractor

It was always good news when I was a young boy to come home from school and see that Dad was working on the home field. Most of our farmland was several miles south of our home place, so Dad's working in the fields took him away from our sight. I was excited to see him in that field because I knew I could get a ride on the tractor when I got my chores completed.

Consequently, when I got home, I followed my regular schedule with one change—tempo. I moved and did things a lot faster to save time for a longer ride. I changed clothes, came downstairs, and gathered around the kitchen table with my mom, sisters, and brother. We visited about the school day while we had our snack. During these days I wasn't in the mood to use the visiting as a means of procrastinating about my responsibilities. Instead I ate quickly, answering Mom's questions between gulps, and ran out the door to tend to the farm animals.

When I finished I walked to meet my father in the field—I did not run because I didn't want to look too excited; that would be the action of a little boy. When I intersected his path, he stopped by putting the clutch in, and the tractor's motor kept running hard. I jumped on; we had work to do, there was no time for casual greetings. I was on the tractor, sitting on a metal shelf between my father's legs, and just that fast, we were moving down the field again.

Once we were going, we had time for talk: How's "Ambroses" (one of the many nicknames my dad had for me)? Did I get the chores done? Any problems? What did I learn in school today? After I answered his questions, I could ask mine, as I tried to act years older than my age and knowledgeable about farming things. Talk was never long; the tractor was loud and made that difficult. Nonetheless I sat there and watched the fields while I bounced back and forth between my father's legs.

I felt a security and comfort sitting there, almost like being within my father's presence. I guess it relaxed me, because it usually didn't take long for me to fall asleep. Dad watched over me while I slept for a while. Eventually, though, he would awaken me and tell me it was time to go home. It may not have lasted long, but it was always one of the joys of being a farmer's son!

> For "In him we live and move and have our being"; as even some of your own poets have said, "For we too are his offspring."
>
> (Acts of the Apostles 17:28)

Breaking Open the Story

This boy is given a sense of identity and responsibility from his father. He will continue to "be" his father's son long after the death of his parent.

- ◆ In what ways have you been affected or formed by your father or father figure?
- ◆ Recall the times and ways you were given a sense of identity and responsibility.
- ◆ This father passed on values and beliefs to his son, even if unconsciously. In what ways do you consciously or unconsciously shape someone's values and beliefs?

More Than Meets the Eye

Here's a moment in the continuing creation of one boy. The ordinary routines of working together, being silent and talking, and nicknaming are all ways the father is shaping his son. These simple actions contribute to the passing of boyhood and the arrival of young manhood. This is possible because the father opens a space in his life for his son, literally and figuratively. The symbolism of "sitting on a metal shelf between my father's legs . . ." speaks loudly to an important point: men are birthed not only by their mothers biologically, men are also "inside" their fathers, who birth them in some very real ways. As a result this son consciously stretches his own understanding of who he is: "I did not run . . . that would be the action of a little boy." He chooses to act and talk beyond his years, for he sees maturity in his father, and he longs to be that way too.

Encounters of this type are life-shaping and holy, for these two people are actively participating with God in a moment of creation. Like most boys his age, this son was practicing how to be grown-up and capable; the field was his classroom and his father was his teacher, teaching the virtues of hard work and responsibility.

Parenting continues for a lifetime in a variety of ways: children are "birthed" into an identity, a lifestyle, a value system, a worldview, perhaps even a trade. These birthings happen almost imperceptibly, and yet they create who and what a person really is. The effects of the good parenting this father is doing very naturally move beyond the immediate family to influence society as a whole. Parents who raise their families in this way create children capable of becoming good neighbors and good citizens.

God is the author of all life. Whenever and wherever creation is taking place, God is present. Thus birthing and parenting (the ongoing nurturing and development of life) are a participation in God's creativity.

Praying

Who we are today has been shaped to some extent by the people around us. Celebrate some of the positive influences who have surrounded you.

1. As always, take two minutes to ready yourself for praying. Sit comfortably, breathe deeply, and relax.

2. Begin by slowly repeating the following sentence at least three times, pausing briefly each time you say it: "Who I am now has been influenced positively by the presence and actions of others."

3. Now repeat the following sentence three times in the same manner, filling in the blanks for yourself: "Who I am today has been influenced by _____ doing _____ with or for me."

4. And finally, gratefully, repeat the following prayer three times in a similar fashion: "Thank you, God, our Father, for birthing me through the actions and presence of these others in my life."

For group praying, one person should lead all in saying together the first and third sentences aloud.

For the second sentence, wherein each person will recall specific individuals and actions particular to him or her, the leader alone should repeat the sentence aloud, pausing at the appropriate places for all to fill in their own blanks.

THE STORY TOLD Teen Alcoholism

When we discovered that Ted was heavily involved with alcohol, it seemed that I was the one who did all the hard work—talking to Ted about counseling, calling his school, talking to parents of his friends and then his friends, searching his room. The emotional aloneness that I felt during those few days was compounded by the experience of "tricking" our son into going to a treatment center and leaving him there, then having him describe me to the counselors as the "bad guy," the one who was always freaking out, and his dad as the cool, understanding one.

> As Christ was anointed Priest, Prophet, and King, so may you live always as a member of his body, sharing everlasting life.
>
> (The Rite of Baptism, no. 98)

Breaking Open the Story

Family living at one time or another seems to require tough loving! Parenting with tough love is painful.

♦ Recall a situation when you had to use tough love. A stance for tough love entails some consequences. It's a decision to say, "I want the good of the other, despite the risks involved for me."

♦ In the situation you recalled, what were the risks you took in tough loving?

More Than Meets the Eye

Ted's mom has described one moment in the history of her family. It is a crisis moment, calling forth tough love. Spiritually speaking, every family event, including a crisis, is a part of the larger family story, which might well be called their particular "salvation history." Salvation history recounts how God actively brings individual members and the human family to a healthy, full life. This history reflects growth in God's image. All have been created "in the image of God . . . male and female he created them" (Genesis 1:27), but periodically we stray from this truth and need to return.

In the Scriptures prophets are those who call people back to "right living" (unlike the popular definition of *prophet* as one who supposedly has psychic abilities). Prophets are those who recognize a problem or evil, name it as such, and then are willing to take any necessary action. Prophets put aside their own fears or personal ambitions in order to focus on the greater good.

Within this domestic church, Mom exercised her baptismal role as prophet in her family's salvation history. Her parental tough love recognized Ted's alcoholism, named it, and took the necessary steps of confrontation, challenging him to embrace once again the fullness of life that is his. Such prophetic action expressed as tough love is responsible parenting, and is holy.

Although prophecy is hard, often lonely, and even thankless at the moment, prophetic parents play a key role in developing capable members of both church and society. With time this mom may begin to celebrate her stance of tough love, knowing that by addressing her son's alcoholism, she serves life, both his and the community's. When parents fail to use tough love as needed, the illness or disease of the family can become a problem requiring society's attention.

As this mother came to know, her call to be prophet has a frightening consequence: prophets are anything but popular! Because no one likes to hear that he or she is on the wrong track or in error, the result for the prophet is often a sense of alienation, as witnessed by Elijah, Jeremiah, and John the Baptizer. Alienation within the home is especially painful, because everyone's lives are so intertwined. This often results in loneliness for the prophet. Like the prophets of old, God is present to this mother in her loneliness, comforting and strengthening her. Like the prophets of old, her prophetic word is God's word, a living word, one that will bear fruit for all.

Praying

The role of the prophet has been stated rather concisely and effectively in a prayer associated with Alcoholics Anonymous. After reflecting on this story of teen alcoholism, it seems most appropriate to pray in solidarity with all who are recovering from this disease.

1. Be seated with your eyes closed, and silence your mind and heart for a few moments.

2. Pray aloud three times the AA Serenity Prayer. Do so slowly and deliberately, listening to your voice pronouncing each word.

> God grant me the serenity to accept the things I cannot change, courage to change the things I can, and wisdom to know the difference. Thy will, not mine, be done.
>
> *(Twelve Steps and Twelve Traditions*, p. 41)

3. Sit quietly after speaking. Pay close attention to any person or situation that may surface in your mind and heart as a result of this prayer.

4. This person or circumstance may need *you* as a prophet!

5. Pray the Serenity Prayer once more, this time with the particular person or situation in mind. Pray that you will

- have the courage to help effect a change if needed
- stand back and accept what does not need your presence
- be wise enough to know the difference

To pray this ritual with a group, arrange for three individuals to speak the AA Serenity Prayer slowly and reflectively. These three should be positioned in different locations, so that the change in voice as well as direction will help others to listen well.

If the group has a sufficient level of trust with one another, when the prayer is finished, provide time for some to share in writing how they may feel called to be a prophet in the life of another. Of course, no names should be given, as anonymity is essential.

THE STORY TOLD Stephen and Dave

Several years ago we brought Dave, a developmentally challenged boy, into our home for foster care. Among the things he had difficulty understanding was history. He could understand the concepts of yesterday and tomorrow, but history was beyond him. I tried talking about cowboys and Indians, industrialization, my great grandfather, and the first Christmas. Nothing worked. He simply couldn't grasp the concept. I started having him watch TV programs that dealt with history. I let him help me paste photographs of my ancestors into a genealogy notebook. I talked about Christopher Columbus.

One evening while we were entertaining guests, Dave ran downstairs from his bath stark naked, ran over to me, and, pointing to his head, he said, "I got it!" "What have you got?" I asked. "History," he said, smiling broadly and tapping his finger to the side of his head. "Stephen, I got history!" "Okay," I said, "explain it to me." He drew back as if to say, "Let there be light," and said: "Before I was born, there was stuff going on. Everything today is born from it. I'm smart!" "Yes, you are," I replied, "but you're also standing naked in the living room in front of company." "Oh, my God," he said, "I forgot I was naked."

Three weeks ago we found two abandoned kittens on our farm. One had a slight limp. "Let's name him I Claudius," he said, "and the other Claudia." "Why those names?" I asked. "Because good Caesar Claudius limped too. It's history." Indeed it is.

> The present moment is an ever-flowing source of holiness. . . .
> The present moment always reveals the presence and the power of God.
>
> (Jean-Pierre de Caussade, *Abandonment to Divine Providence*, pp. 49–50)

Breaking Open the Story

Even though this story is funny, it is also quite touching. Here, the ultimate joy lies in the sharing between Stephen and Dave over a long-time-in-coming accomplishment.

- ♦ What are some of the simple (and sometimes tedious) ways that you nurture others to grow and mature?
- ♦ When have you taken delight in an accomplishment of one of your family members?

More Than Meets the Eye

Stephen has spent considerable time, energy, and a variety of techniques trying to teach Dave the concept of history. For Dave, grasping history is another aspect of developing into a mature adult. This story celebrates the final moment of breakthrough, when *history* is comprehended. What a joyous, exciting moment it is!

Looking deeper, when Stephen and his guests hear of Dave's insight about history, they actually experience him growing, developing, and maturing. Ordinary moments of education are really moments of creation. This developmentally challenged child will be able to contribute to society in a more meaningful way because of the deep dedication, repeated teaching, and patient persistence of his foster father. Dave's breakthrough reveals the creative power found constantly in all of life. That creative presence is none other than the power of God.

The simplest learning experience or shared accomplishment, such as this one, can become a celebration of the presence of God for those who understand one fact: God consistently and persistently shapes us through those who love us. Here, Stephen is an instrument of God, true to his role as foster parent.

Real expressions of God's creative presence abound in all families, though at first glance these may appear rather routine, mundane, or in cases such as this, even humorous. The task at hand is to cooperate with God's ongoing creation in, around, and through us.

Praying

Some writing paper and a pen may be useful in the following prayer.

1. Sit comfortably, and with your eyes closed, breathe deeply for a few moments.

2. Call to mind someone you know who is currently learning a task, studying a particularly difficult subject, or working toward an accomplishment.

3. List the names of those who are teaching or cooperating in this person's accomplishment. Recall how each is contributing to this experience of learning. Include yourself if this applies.

4. Reflect and visualize God's creative power in this instance—through these people—in this process of learning.

5. Pray the following simple prayer, speaking the name of each person recalled as well as the particular gift each has contributed (for example, carpentry, patience, persistence). Let your prayer become a "litany of thanksgiving" for people, for gifts shared, and for the creative process of learning.

> Thank you, God, for _____,
> to whom you have given the gift of _____,
> and who has shared it so generously for the benefit of others!

6. As you close your litany, add, "Together, we give you praise, Creator God, for allowing us to participate in your creative power."

To pray this ritual as a group, paper and pens will be necessary. Follow the ritual as outlined until step 5. Encourage all in the group to pray their litany of thanksgiving together softly. This prayer of "murmuring"—many people speaking different words simultaneously—takes on the character of gentle rain falling in many places at the same time. When the murmuring subsides, invite everyone to close this litany by praying together the words of step 6.

THE STORIES TOLD Facing Disappointments

Watching our son, tall and handsome in his basketball uniform, filled me with parental pride. He had given his all to this team, including daily practice after school and lawn-mowing money spent on special shoes. He had worked hard to make the A team and was proud to be associated with a winning team at a winning school.

He was not prepared—nor were we—for the increasingly disappointing sequence of events that followed in his sophomore year. In the first big game, he played almost an entire half. His strength was being a team player, passing the ball for inside shots and snatching rebounds from the opposition. He scored six points in that game and was happy with himself—not needing to be a star player, but always in the action, hustling.

In the second game of the season, his playing time decreased to part of a quarter. In succeeding games his playing time decreased again, and by the fifth game of the season, he was getting only "garbage" time at the end of games.

He continued to show up for practice daily, work out regularly, and support the team, but inside he was crushed and angry at the coach. He ended the season depressed and disappointed about the situation. Though we assured him that it was his dedication to the team, his unfailing fidelity to practice, and his ability to encourage other players that was important to us, he was inconsolable. His slumped shoulders, as he sat on the bench, are indelibly etched in my memory.

When Dan's first real love "dumped" him, he stopped in at my office two or three times without calling. The first couple of times, I was not in, but the third time he came, I was there. He sat down and told me that he had something to tell me. He took a letter from his pocket and let me read what she had written to him— a very gentle and kind good-bye. His eyes filled with tears, and we visited for some time. Although his being was wrapped in pain for several months thereafter, I experienced a closeness and intimacy with my nineteen-year-old son that I had not experienced during his earlier teen years. I felt affirmed that my bumbling parenting had somehow been more okay than I'd imagined, and I felt very pleased that Dan's problem-solving and coping skills included a visit with me.

> Everything we call a trial, a sorrow . . .
> believe me . . . the gift is there,
> and the wonder of an overshadowing presence.
> Our joys too conceal diviner gifts.
>
> (Fra Giovanni, 1513)

Breaking Open the Stories

Life is not always fair. Disappointments, rejections, and failures come in many shapes and sizes.

♦ When and where did you first learn that life is not always fair?

Coping is much easier when the burden is shared. Dan's mother gives him a listening ear and heart; the parents of the basketball player reassure him that what really matters is "his dedication to the team, his unfailing fidelity to practice, and his ability to encourage other players."

♦ Who has been a support for you when you have had difficult times?

♦ What did they do for you that was helpful?

More Than Meets the Eye

These parents were able to ease the harshness of life by accompanying their sons through moments of pain. Note that they do not solve nor take away life's difficulties, they only walk with their children.

In a culture that avoids or anesthetizes pain, it is difficult to appreciate the place of suffering. Jesus' life was filled with rejection and unfairness, leading him through a cycle of pain, dying, and rising to new life, a cycle that is referred to as the paschal mystery. In order to arrive at the victory and joy of Easter Sunday, Jesus passed through a Thursday agony in the garden, a Good Friday nailing to the cross and his death, and a Holy Saturday of entombed waiting.

Family living is filled with these same movements in every generation. Mentoring children through this paschal mystery seems easy during their Easters, those times when they are a basketball star, when they have a good relationship with a girlfriend, and so on. But it is difficult for parents to enter into the pain of their own children in their Good Fridays of sitting on the bench, dying to play; in their Holy Saturdays, entombed in the devastation of being dumped by a girl. To accompany someone through life's harsher moments is to show that person a face of God, who is with us always. These parents reassured their sons verbally and nonverbally (by still attending those games) that they valued and loved their sons for who they are, not for what they produced.

Understandably, the first reaction of some parents is to "rescue" their children by intervening, making excuses, blaming the coach or the former girlfriend. The parents in these stories, however, performed the simple acts that lie at the very heart of loving: although others may abandon you, I will not. In doing so they mirror the Father's unconditional love for Jesus as Jesus moved through the rhythm of the paschal mystery.

Praying

For this prayerful reflection, you will need a treasured ring in hand. The ring should have some deep meaning for you; it might be a wedding band or an heirloom passed on for generations. If you are currently wearing it, take it off so you can hold it in your hand.

1. Be seated with the ring in hand, and take a few moments to calm your inner being.

2. Holding your ring between two fingers, first reflect on rings in general:

- how they are unbroken circles
- how each has no beginning or end point
- why rings are considered symbols of love and commitment

3. Look closely at this particular ring. Notice any imperfections, such as scratches, tarnish, or missing stones.

4. Take note: Despite its imperfections, you still cherish this ring; otherwise you would not have selected it for meditation.

5. Renew your fidelity to family with the following prayer:

> Lord, like this ring
> that I continue to treasure,
> even though scratched and imperfect,
> so do I cherish my family,
> with all their disappointments and mistakes.
> Lord, like this ring
> that I would never dream of throwing away,
> so do I remain steadfast in dedication to my family.
> And Lord, as this ring, despite its years of use and wear,
> still communicates beauty and wholeness,
> so do I love my family in their Easter joys,
> their Good Friday pains, and their Holy Saturday entombments.
> Lord, with this ring
> I seek to be an ongoing symbol of faithful love
> in every aspect of your ever unfolding paschal mystery in my
>   family.
> Amen.

When praying this ritual with a group, copies of the prayer of fidelity (from step 5) should be made ahead of time. As the prayer is to begin, invite everyone in the group to take off one of his or her rings, the one most treasured. If some participants do not wear a ring, ask them to pair themselves with someone who does. During step 4 the one with a ring may share reflections about why it is so cherished with the one who does not have a ring. The final prayer should be spoken slowly in unison.

THE STORY TOLD The First Day of Kindergarten

His backpack rested heavily on his narrow shoulders. He stood there, dressed in his "first day of school" best, looking half his tender age and acting twice as old.

"Do you have everything," I asked. ". . . lunch, Kleenex, pencil, and so on?" "Did you use the bathroom?" "Let me run a comb through your hair once more." His response to my fussing was quiet tolerance. He showed no signs of fear, no whining or tears about his first day of school, all signs of healthy self-reliance. He was ready for his first day of school . . . maybe more ready than I was.

When I announced that it was time to leave, ushering him and his older brother to the car, he protested, "I want to walk to school with the big kids, Mommy," he said. "Walk?" I countered in surprise. "Why, it's your first day. I will take you to your new classroom and make sure you find your teacher, just like I did with your brother, Kory. You might not know where to go or where to hang your coat," I insisted. "No, Mommy, I want to walk with Kory and the neighbor kids."

I did not insist. I kissed him gently and put on a pretend smile of excitement to match his. With a mixture of gratitude and grief, I waved them down the walk until he was out of sight.

> It belongs to the center of the Christian message that children are not properties to own and rule over, but gifts to cherish and care for. Our children are our most important guests, who enter into our home, ask for careful attention, stay for a while and then leave to follow their own way.
>
> (Henri J. M. Nouwen, *Reaching Out*, p. 81)

Breaking Open the Story

For most families the first day of school is both exciting and anxious.

- ♦ Can you identify with the emotions of this story, or were your reactions and those of your child very different?

- ♦ What do you see happening in this kindergartner as he prepares for school?
- ♦ What thoughts and feelings would you imagine this mother is experiencing?

More Than Meets the Eye

Although many parents would not see this as a "holy" moment, sending this boy to kindergarten is really a celebration of this family's efforts to form a self-reliant, responsible citizen, which is an essential task of the Christian family.

Healthy parenting gives each child both "roots and wings." That is to say, there needs to be a balance between nurturance, support, and protection (rootedness), and self-assertion and independence (wings). When such a balance is achieved and maintained, a kind of "holy tension" emerges. It's the tension between support and independence, between holding on and letting go. This kind of parenting reflects how God, with perfect wisdom, treats each of us.

When this tension is in balance, it avoids "unholy" extremes: too much support can lead to overprotection, codependency, smothering; too much independence can result in irresponsibility, resentment, and disrespect. It is a difficult, delicate balance to maintain, and requires Godlike wisdom.

Apparently this mother has rooted her son well since birth. Even now she wants to take care of the things that might help him feel secure. But her son wants to try his own wings. The many moments of rooting in the past five-plus years have developed a good, strong sense of independence in this child, now ready to fly.

His leave-taking causes Mom some anxiety, for mothering this child is turning out differently than with her first son. Mom cannot launch, discipline, clothe, or play with both children in exactly the same way. A consistency of basic values and rules in the household is necessary, but she (and all parents) comes to understand and appreciate that each of her children is unique.

Parental sensitivity to a child's uniqueness mirrors God's relationship with us. Although we are all loved unconditionally, God relates to each of us according to our particular needs, problems, gifts, and weaknesses. As such, Moms and Dads make adjustments in their parenting, which are the ongoing "spiritual exercises" of parenthood.

Praying

This ritual is simple: Repeat the following adaptation of the Serenity Prayer from Alcoholics Anonymous. If it is helpful, make a copy of this prayer and carry it with you or post it in a prominent place so that you might pray it often.

> Lord, grant me the serenity to "root" those who are rightly dependent on me, to encourage those whose "wings" need to fly, and to have the wisdom to accept the holy tension created between the two. Amen.

For ritualizing with a group, make sure copies of the adapted Serenity Prayer are prepared ahead of time for all members to pray together. Encourage folks to take it home, carry it with them, post it prominently, and so on.

THE STORY TOLD
The Spirit—Timeless Yet Ever New

For the life of me, I could not see the connection between pop cans and my son's Confirmation class. When I was confirmed, we memorized a lot of stuff, things like the seven deadly sins and the cardinal virtues. We visited a nursing home once and learned about the gifts of the Holy Spirit, which we thought came when the bishop slapped us on the cheek.

What recycling paper and pop cans and picking up trash in the park had to do with the Holy Spirit was beyond me until his Confirmation project was completed.

I found it awfully irritating to be lectured by my adolescent son for throwing a gum wrapper out the window, or for using an aerosol can of lubricant on a sticking door. He kept telling me, with righteousness, that everyone was responsible for taking care of the earth, preserving its natural resources. In all honesty, during those months before Confirmation, I found out more about biodegradable products and consumer consumption than I ever wanted to know.

Here was my son, the kid who had to be bribed to take out the trash, standing guard over the three bins he himself designed for recycling trash, jumping on his sister for dropping a piece of plastic wrap in with the glass jars. Only an adolescent could bring such fanaticism to a Confirmation project.

When his brother and sister could take no more, he gave long talks about how it was everyone's duty to save the earth, not just a few people picking up after everybody else. His mother and I would have been just as happy if he had managed to save his room, but his mission became far too expansive to spend time picking up his own clothes.

I really wasn't convinced that he was making any connections with the sacrament until he took "Francis" as his Confirmation name. He explained to me that Francis of Assisi showed great reverence for the earth and all its creatures.

The whole experience of preparing for Confirmation turned into his chance to be responsible, to be the one initiating some new action to better our world. He grew up a lot that year; I think I did too!

> If you know what you are looking for, you will never see what you do not expect to find.
>
> (An artist, as quoted by Bill Moyers in
> *Weavings*, November–December 1994, p. 37)

Breaking Open the Story

Take note of the different emphases in Confirmation preparation from father to son.

♦ What are some of the generational differences in religious formation you have noticed?

Despite the tension and resentment expressed in the beginning of the story, this sacramental preparation ended on a positive note. And significantly, it was positive for both child and parent.

♦ Recall some examples of learning through your child's religious formation.

More Than Meets the Eye

Confirmation preparation should have been pretty cut-and-dried for this son and his entire family. However, a different and interesting kind of process began to unfold in this family. The spirit of God was active not only in this child but also in this family through the child.

Dad was honest enough to admit feeling "awfully irritated," and his reaction was not so unusual. When thrown into new situations, most of us feel uncomfortable and upset. Recall the following passage from John:

> The wind blows where it chooses, and you hear the sound of it, but you do not know where it comes from or where it goes. So it is with everyone who is born of the Spirit.
>
> (3:8)

It would seem that the Spirit constantly surprises, that is, blows people into situations we might never have imagined or chosen ourselves . . . as this dad came to find out.

As children prepare for sacraments, their family and parish are invited to renew their faith also. In this instance the Spirit has surprisingly expanded this whole family's understanding of what it means to reverence the earth. Good disciples are also good stewards of creation.

This story demonstrates vividly how religious traditions are ever new, how unchanging truths are ever fresh in the present. This boy's Confirmation became a link between the traditional teachings about the gifts of the Holy Spirit and the religious values of stewardship and justice. This father began to understand that recycling and reverencing the earth can be Spirit-filled actions. One and the same Spirit worked through the man of Assisi centuries ago and lives now in this young "Francis."

Praying

When asked the question, "What would you save if your home was threatened with fire?" people invariably respond by saying "family photo albums." Take one of your albums of family pictures to your place of prayer.

1. Sit comfortably, perhaps with a refreshing drink at your side.

2. Spend a leisurely half hour leafing through your family's album, reveling in your ancestors and times past. Do so with a mind-set, the "spirit-set," to identify positive characteristics or virtues that have consistently been lived by your family, generation after generation. For example, notice such traits as honesty, hospitality, humor in the face of disaster, and so on, manifested in the lives of various relatives.

3. Consider the question, In what way (even surprisingly) has this same value or virtue been shown in your own family, even to this day?

4. Spend a few moments thanking God for this trait, a genuine "heirloom of family faith." And now that you have become

aware of this gift, seek to share it with others in new and creative ways.

5. Remember the words of Peter at the gate of the Temple, called the Beautiful Gate: "I have no silver or gold, but what I have I give you" (Acts of the Apostles 3:6).

When offering this prayer in a group setting, the leader will need to prepare. He or she should pray this ritual at home in advance, focusing on one virtue or positive characteristic found within his or her own family. Then for the group gathering, the leader should bring pictures of relatives and friends who exemplify the revealed characteristic, showing the photos and speaking of instances when this virtue was shown. (In effect, the leader models this ritual for the group.) The leader then invites the group to recollect individually, noticing virtues of their own family members. After an appropriate amount of quiet time, folks are asked to share these with others seated around them.

The final words from the Acts of the Apostles (in step 5) should be the source of meditation for the group. This preparation may lead to fruitful reflection later.

THE STORY TOLD The Witness

Even though it happened in 1970, I'll never forget the brave, petite housewife and mother, an assembly-line worker, who gave such powerful witness to her Gospel beliefs.

It was during the height of the Vietnam War, and she spoke for no more than five minutes or so at a peace rally. The company she worked for transferred her to the fragmentation bomb assembly line. She asked for another assignment, but was refused, being told in effect, "You will work where we put you or you will not have a job here."

With a large family, her paycheck was definitely needed, but her conscience bothered her, what with the prospect of building bombs that would maim and kill innocent civilians.

She spoke of her husband's support, and how difficult it was for them to make their decision, forced by an over-the-weekend deadline. She (and her family) accepted unemployment, choosing to sacrifice financially rather than compromise their principles.

A number of nationally known speakers were at that rally, but I've forgotten their names and words long ago. This woman, this family, who laid their own security on the line, I will never forget.

> "Blessed is the womb that bore you and the breasts that nursed you!" But he said, "Blessed rather are those who hear the word of God and obey it!"
>
> (Luke 11:27–28)

Breaking Open the Story

One remarkable aspect of this story is that the "brave, petite house-wife and mother, an assembly-line worker" is still remembered so many years later. Why? Because her message was not merely words and ideas.

- ♦ Recall such dedicated persons in your life. What are their convictions?

♦ On what principles would you and your family take a stand such as the one taken by the family in the story?

More Than Meets the Eye

The extraordinary power of this woman's message is rooted in the ordinariness with which she and her family chose to live out their commitment to social justice. Not everyone is an articulate, gifted speaker. However, each person, every household, gives witness, knowingly or unknowingly, to a particular set of values: good, bad, or indifferent. Here, one household (that of the speaker and her family) challenges another household (that of this story's author) to re-examine life and how it is to be lived. Together the speaker's family made a decision, supported it, and ultimately paid the consequences for it. Their lived action witnessed to their Christian principles.

In the Scriptures when Jesus said to his disciples: "You are the light of the world. A city built on a hill cannot be hid" (Matthew 5:14), he taught that the values and concerns of each person and every family do "shine" brightly for others to see. This woman spoke of her family's priority, one different from that of the status quo. Although economic security can be a strong force when measuring the "success" of family, this family knew that financial well-being was not the only criterion! Providing for their immediate family needed to be balanced with the good of the human family. This woman, speaking for her family, became "light of the world," calling society to consider a different way.

God does call all families to help transform society; how that call will be put into practice will differ for each. Not every family is called to give up employment to further a cause. Some families may support social justice by sharing financial resources with appropriate organizations; some may educate themselves (and through them, others) by attending conferences and classes; still others may send a family member into full-time ministry at home or abroad. For this family their witness required searching for another job, perhaps buying fewer clothes, eating simpler meals, all ordinary enough tasks in and of themselves.

History shows us that the choice for unemployment did not stop a war. Whether or not you agree politically with the stance taken by this woman and her family, there is no mistaking the value of her witness as she spoke with such conviction. In this family's attempt to translate their Christian values into daily living, they sought to bring forth a holiness in themselves as well as others, contributing to "a kingdom of truth and life, a kingdom of holiness and grace, a kingdom of justice, love, and peace" (*The Sacramentary*, from the preface for the feast of Christ the King).

Praying

An *examen* involves the regular, conscious act of honestly looking at ourselves and the way we live. We seek to notice the presence and activity of God, and to question ourselves as to how well or how poorly we react to God's call.

1. Begin with a prayerful posture, whether seated, kneeling, or in any position that helps you to reflect. Take two minutes or so to calm down, letting go of any concerns and thoughts; create a mental space for God to lead you.

2. Read the following anonymous question slowly, thoughtfully: If Christianity was against the law, and you were arrested, accused of being Christian, would there be enough evidence to convict you?

3. Ask the holy spirit of our God to guide your reflection. Pray along these lines:

Spirit of the Living God, deep within me,
you know me through and through.
Bring to my mind and heart those happenings and circumstances
you wish me to consider.

4. Start your examen with these questions; take as much time as you are led to for reflection.

Is there evidence of me witnessing Christian values . . .

- in my workplace?
- at home?
- in my recreation?
- in the way I use my money?

5. Close by thanking God for any insights you may have received, and for the challenge to better live your faith.

If this ritual is to be prayed with a group, prepare copies of the following for all members:

If Christianity was against the law, and I was arrested, accused of being a Christian, would there be enough evidence to convict me . . .

- in my workplace?
- at home?
- in my recreation?
- in the way I use my money?

As the prayer unfolds, allow a specified length of time (perhaps fifteen minutes) for everyone to reflect silently on the previous question. Encourage people to find a quiet spot: take a short walk, visit the church or chapel if it is near at hand, and so on. Then gather for a common thanksgiving to God.

———◆———

CHAPTER 4

Sharing the Church's Mission

Throughout the centuries, family has been called "the domestic church." As church the family shares in the mission of the larger church: worshiping, evangelizing, catechizing, and serving. Family living, in its everyday activities and relationships, is intended to be a mirror image of our membership in God's larger family. Such basics as bathing, feeding, and clothing the family are essential experiences, helping us to understand how God loves unconditionally, providing for all.

In both communities of believers, the Creator God gives life, the Son heals and forgives, and the Spirit empowers people to seek and find God in their love of and care for one another.

Though the domestic church and the larger church are unique, the two are complementary and radically interdependent.

THE STORY TOLD "Picking Up" Prayer

Daniel is getting into everything, and is learning something new every day. Last week he began willingly to wave and to hug good-bye, though he still looks disappointed when his daddy leaves.

Tonight at dinner Daniel watched intently as we held hands to pray grace. He even stopped his two-fisted eating to take us in with his eyes while we said the "Bless us, O Lord" after our thanksgiving prayers. He even tried the sign of the cross by himself, and Tom and Vic snickered to themselves at their ten-month-old brother's version.

> By prayer let us understand any expression of our relationship to God done under the influence of the Holy Spirit . . . to raise our hearts and minds toward our Father.
> (Richard J. Hauser, *In His Spirit*, pp. 41 and 44)

Breaking Open the Story

Daniel is doing what his family does in order to be like them. Long before he can possibly understand what these gestures mean, he begins to imitate what he sees around him.

- How and by whom were you taught to pray?
- What are the ways your family prays together?

More Than Meets the Eye

Daniel imitates the actions of those around him, unaware of the meaning behind their gestures and words. Like Daniel, most children "pick up" prayer while observing, then imitating, their own family at prayer. In a very real sense, praying is more "caught" than taught.

Like most acquired skills and arts, learning how to pray develops in stages. Up to ten months old, Daniel showed no interest in or awareness of his family's ritual of praying grace at meals. He continued eating from the moment he got into his chair, through the grace, until he was finished. But now at this age, Mom notices that Daniel has stopped eating and is somehow attentive to what the others are doing. He begins to participate in his own way, moving his hand trying to imitate their touches to forehead, chest, and shoulders. Daniel is learning to pray by learning to pray with—learning by imitation! A consistent repetition of the same ritual will slowly but surely teach him to pray. In fact, this type of consistency is a key element in developing all prayer. Only later will he be taught the actual meaning of this ritual gesture, with its accompanying words.

Part of the mission of the church-at-large is to be a praying community. The church depends on the family to teach its members the ways of prayer, beginning with the simplest of gestures and most basic of attitudes. At the same time, the larger church also invites and teaches the family to participate in the church's rituals and common prayer, drawing the family into a fuller experience of God's presence.

Both Daniel's uncoordinated sign of the cross and the rituals of Sunday worship are ways of raising our heart and mind toward the Father. The prayer found in both communities is vital, and is necessarily linked to the other.

Praying

1. Sit quietly for a few moments, relaxing, opening yourself to whatever God might choose to bring to your mind and heart in this time of prayer.

2. Recall the first prayer you ever learned; remember some of the words if you can. Picture yourself saying that prayer: the setting, the time of day, the people present, and any other surrounding details. Enter the memory fully.

3. Recall too the fervor and devotion that you had as a child when you prayed this particular prayer. Tap into those feelings for a few moments.

4. Now pray that same prayer, doing so with the childlike attitude you just remembered and felt.

5. Ask God for the grace to recapture that attitude of your childhood prayer, though now in an adult way.

> Loving God,
> I come to you like a child before a caring parent.
> I open my hands to whatever you have for me today.
> I kneel (or sit) with confidence,
> for you hold me in your presence,
> you listen to my fumbling words,
> you even hear the movement of my heart without words.
> Renew in me
> the simple faith of a child,
> a sense of wonder at all creation,
> an attitude of gratitude for all that is,
> a peaceful spirit in times of trouble,
> a joyful heart in times of goodness.
> Send your spirit to pray in me
> as I raise my heart and mind to you. Amen.

When praying as a group, in addition to reciting the preceding prayer, invite the participants to make up their own prayer. It should be one that also has a "sing-songy" rhyme scheme, capturing a childlike sense of fun, even in prayer—maybe especially in prayer! If the group meets regularly, have all these prayers copied and distributed at your next gathering.

THE STORY TOLD Taking Care of Grandma

My grandmother died a couple of months before her ninety-fifth birthday. She had been in a nursing home for six months, following a serious stroke that left her partially paralyzed and unable to speak.

For several years her five children, all retired, had taken turns spending most of the day at Grandma's apartment—cooking for her, visiting, helping her maintain a measure of independence. During the last six months of her life, they took turns spending much of each day assisting in her care at the nursing facility.

It was fortunate that there were five children able to share the responsibility for my grandmother's care. It took a lot of cooperation, coordination, and sacrifices. In those last months, my father, his brothers, and his sister were on the phone with each other almost nightly—discussing, comforting, reassuring. It took constant attention and effort to keep a family (in this case, a family of families) functioning as a unit.

> Taking part in the common life means dwelling in a web of relationships, the many threads tugging at you while also holding you upright.
>
> (Scott Russell Sanders, "The Web of Life,"
> in *Utne Reader*, March–April 1995, p. 70)

Breaking Open the Story

This granddaughter shares with us a rather straightforward account of the last years and months of her grandmother's life. Her grandmother's five children chose to visit, cook for, and help in her extended caregiving.

- ♦ In what ways have you and your extended family rallied together to help someone who was vulnerable or in need of care?

More Than Meets the Eye

The mission of the church has always included a sensitivity to and care for those people most vulnerable: poor, infirm, unborn, elderly, physically or mentally challenged people. As a result the church has opened hospitals, orphanages, nursing facilities, and so on, calling for care for those in need.

This granddaughter tells us how her "family of families" adopts this same mission and ministry for one of their own. The chores these five children performed—spending most of the day at Grandma's apartment, cooking for her, visiting with her, helping her maintain a measure of independence—are vivid examples of domestic ministry.

Unlike the larger church, both parish and universal, this type of home ministry is seldom recognized or affirmed in any official way. But there is little doubt that such actions are holy. As this grand-daughter points out, the personal schedules of her father, aunt, and uncles needed to be coordinated, and sacrifices had to be made. The dispassionate manner in which this story is told may indicate that this family of families lived with a very basic assumption: We are family; we take care of one another, especially the one who is most in need.

In addition to the care of their mother, these brothers and sister are comforting and reassuring one another on a daily basis. This too is a form of domestic ministry. Throughout the ups and downs of the illness, these family members were on the phone with each other almost nightly. This family, when not doing something for their mother, was being a source of support for one another.

The care and commitment of this family were not thought of as extraordinary or worthy of praise; the family just did it.

> After [Jesus] had washed their feet . . . he said to them, . . . "If I, your Lord and Teacher, have washed your feet, you also ought to wash one another's feet. For I have set you an example, that you also should do as I have done to you."
>
> (John 13:12–15)

Praying

You will need some writing paper or a blank notecard or the like, plus an envelope, for this prayer time.

1. Call to mind a member of your family or circle of friends who currently requires the ongoing care of another.

2. Ask God for the grace to see this person who needs such assistance as a "treasure to be cared for" rather than as a "burden to be carried." You might begin by praying the following:

Lord, you are the creator of all life;
You make everyone and everything for goodness.
Even though _____ is now unable to care completely for self,
_____ is still a priceless treasure causing me to . . .

3. Write and send an encouraging note to the family member, friend, or neighbor who is currently a caregiver to this one in need. Affirm the person for the seldom recognized "domestic ministry of care" that she or he is extending on a regular basis.

When ritualizing in a group, make sure that enough writing material and envelopes are available for all participants. As the notes are written, encourage the group to visit with others, telling stories of the domestic minister of care they are writing to.

THE STORY TOLD Benjamin's Baptism

I remember Benjamin's Baptism; he was born nine years after my youngest sister—we called him the caboose. Benjamin cried now and then throughout his Baptism. It wasn't a loud wailing but kind of a whimpering. Maybe he was just complaining about the temperature of the water and all the fussing over him. As his oldest sister, I helped Mom bathe him, apply lotion, and dress him before church. And people photographed him and begged him for smiles all morning.

There was some murmuring by my relatives and friends as Mom and Dad and Ben's godparents were asked some questions by the deacon at the beginning of the ceremony. Then all of us sisters, brothers, and cousins were invited by the priest to come up around the font so the little ones could see better. We watched him pour water on Ben from a large pitcher, then anoint him with some oil. He lit a small candle from the Easter one and gave it to Dad. Then Father held Benjamin in his hands and said to everyone at Mass, "This is our newest member, Benjamin Michael," and we all clapped.

I could tell Grandma and Grandpa were happy with all the aunts, uncles, and others who came. After church we all went to our house for dinner, with presents and champagne toasts (7-Up for the kids) wishing Ben good health, happiness, and lots of blessings. Everyone got to hold Benjamin in his long white baptismal gown, the one Grandma bought for her own children, and that all of us twelve cousins have worn.

Lots of pictures were taken, everyone wanting one taken with Ben. And there was storytelling, especially funny ones from Uncle Stan, about the silly things Dad and my uncles and aunts did when they were growing up.

Too bad Benjamin fell asleep after dinner and missed all the fun. We all said this big day was for Benjamin, but I know inside it was for all of us too. It's our way of celebrating another new life in our family. That's the way we've done it for every one of my cousins.

The point of ritual is not to make magic, to dominate someone
or something and make it bend to our will, but to make a divine
connection, to experience a momentary unity of the two worlds.

(Robert A. Johnson, *Ecstasy*, p. 83)

Breaking Open the Story

This is a snapshot of one family with their newborn. Baptisms, along
with hospital visits, baby showers, and a variety of other activities,
welcome a newborn into the family.

♦ What are the traditional ways your family celebrates a new
baby?

♦ In what ways are your family's celebration and the church's
ritual of Baptism related?

More Than Meets the Eye

All the picture-taking of Benjamin tries to capture the gift he really
is. This and all the other traditional ways of fussing are really family
rituals that welcome Ben into the family.

This gathering of grandparents, aunts and uncles, cousins and
friends, in the parish church and at home demonstrates how Benjamin is an important part of their lives, a member of this family,
this church. From day one these close relationships contribute to
Ben's well-being. But it does not stop there; family relationships are
irreplaceable for Benjamin's spiritual growth too. He will come to
understand God's love and care through the acceptance and support shown by this living, flesh-and-blood family.

Family customs and church rituals complement each other and
are dependent on each other. The actions and traditions of Benjamin's family help us to understand the church's baptismal celebration. Benjamin was fussed over at home: bathed and dressed,
passed around and held, toasted and photographed countless times.
Such rituals express this family's belief that Benjamin is a priceless
gift. The church's rituals provide deeper insight into the significance
of the family celebration. White garments, anointing with sacred

oils, an Easter candle, and blessed water are all part of the fuss God's family makes when initiating new members into the Body of Christ. Baptism is a reflection of what needs to be remembered in the home: respecting the dignity of life, seeing the giftedness and sacredness of new life, and knowing that we are forgiven and loved by our God.

A holy mirroring and interdependence exists between the family as domestic church and the larger parish community. Benjamin is, in fact, sacred to both his family and his church. It is right that both should fuss over him. The partying and sacramenting in both communities reflects God's work and presence.

Praying

For this prayer time, you will need a photograph that shows "my family, my clan, my church." It might have been taken at your own birth or Baptism, or at the time of some other significant event as family gathered together for you. In addition you will need a sheet of paper and a pen or pencil. Have both items ready before proceeding.

1. Open a space for God by pausing for two minutes. In this brief time, close your eyes and focus all your inner attention on the air moving in and out of your lungs, your chest rising and falling with each breath.

2. Open your eyes. Now hold your photo and look closely at the faces of each person in the picture. For each person, ask yourself these questions:

- How am I special to him or her?
- What would he or she say to God in thanksgiving for me?

3. List these thoughts briefly in a column on your paper. This becomes a litany of thanks for the "gift to others" God has made you!

4. Put the photo down and hold your list in front of you. Reread it from top to bottom, saying, "Thanks be to God" after each item. You are indeed wondrously made, in the image and likeness of our God!

If this prayer is to be shared in a group, one person should serve as leader, bringing a personal photo from her or his family. After the leader talks about the impressions of thanks to God for two or three family members, she or he invites all others to recall a picture of their own gathered family. In a period of quiet, each member of the group should write her or his litany of thanks based on those remembered in their photos.

The leader draws this common prayer to a close by asking everyone to share one of his or her "thanks" in litany with all others. After each has spoken, the group responds, "Thanks be to God!"

THE STORIES TOLD Mending Tears

My husband had died by the time Nick was a senior in high school. Nick had a darling girlfriend whom we all liked. But I worried about the seriousness of their relationship, so Nick and I had a talk about it. I voiced my concern about pregnancy and what that could mean in his life. He assured me that it wasn't a problem. So when he came to me and told me Judy was pregnant, I was angry and hurt. I can't remember what was said, but things soon cooled down and life went on. Judy's mom made her a special dress for senior prom, we had a baby shower, and I felt everything was in place. Wrong!

One day as I was rushing off to a prework meeting, Nick stopped me in the doorway and said, "Judy doesn't feel welcome here; you make her feel uncomfortable." He was really angry and lashing out at me. Full of frustration because I felt I had handled the whole thing pretty well, I said, "Nick, what more do you want from me?" and stormed out the front door because I was running late.

After I had driven about ten blocks, the anger, tears, and frustration were replaced with a great sense of sadness and a longing to understand. I turned the car around and went back home. I went to him and said, "Nick, for the things I've said and done that have hurt you so much, I am so sorry." He just grabbed me and held on and cried his heart out. It wasn't that he was so angry as that he was scared and didn't know what to do next.

***

Our eight-year-old son was preparing for his first confession and first Holy Communion. He was a pretty normal second grader. He liked to ride his bike, build Lego ships, and had his share of hassles with his younger brother.

As he learned about the sacrament of Reconciliation, we learned about it also, through his take-home materials from school. We were somewhat concerned that he didn't understand the whole idea of God's unconditional love and forgiveness, and the necessity of being genuinely sorry for something. We seriously considered holding him back a year or two (which parents were allowed to do at that time if they thought a child wasn't mature enough for Reconciliation).

Then one morning my opinion of his readiness changed completely. He came down to the kitchen for breakfast before school wearing a jelly-stained shirt. I told him to go change immediately, but he insisted that it was all right to wear the shirt to school today because the jelly was there yesterday and no one had said anything. We got into a big argument, and I sent him back to his room in tears to change.

When he came back down, he approached me from behind, put his arms around my waist, and said he was sorry for talking back. I was still steaming, and I told him sternly to hurry up or he'd miss his ride to school.

He stood right in front of me, looked me square in the eye, and said, "Mommy, you have to forgive me because you love me."

> Repentance and mutual pardon within the bosom of the Christian family, so much a part of daily life, receive their specific sacramental expression in Christian penance.
> (Pope John Paul II, *Familiaris Consortio*, no. 58)

Breaking Open the Stories

Sometimes it's little things, sometimes it's major issues, but whatever the reason, rare is the family without conflicts that isolate and separate one member from another. Nick's mom and the eight-year-old make the first movement toward reconciliation in these stories.

+ Recall a recent conflict in your family. If it has been reconciled, how did it take place? If it has not been reconciled, what obstacles are in the way?

More Than Meets the Eye

Family life is like a fabric intricately woven together. Just as a fabric's strength and pattern are the direct result of the weaving process, so are family members woven together by the threads of daily living:

joys and sorrows, successes and failures. The fabric of home life has its share of rips and holes, some small like jelly-stained shirts, some major and complex like teen pregnancy. The families in these stories are practicing the mending of tears as they happen, taking part in the ongoing repair work.

Breaking relationships, or sin, divides, for it tears the very fabric of household life. On the other hand, forgiveness and reconciliation mend the rips in that fabric. Just as in sewing, reconciliation strengthens the material of family life with the additional threads used to bring about the repair. These families actively show that no one is ever too young or too old to initiate the needlework, that no issue is so large or so small that it cannot be patched.

This mending is completed in two movements: adopting a right attitude and then acting on it.

The right attitude: Nick's mother and the eight-year-old son, whether or not they were consciously aware of it, realized that their relationship with the other person is more important than the issue involved. When they distanced themselves from each other, they gained a different perspective, motivating them to talk through difficult issues and to reconcile. These two stand in the posture of desiring reconciliation: doing all that is necessary to move the process forward.

Acting on this right attitude: Nick's mother turned her car around and reconnected with her son; the child persisted by challenging his mom to forgive him, not once but twice.

The two movements of right attitude and action are holy because they are ultimately the work of God's grace. Nick's mother and the eight-year-old cooperated with God in mending the fabric of family. God's grace is the thread with which the fabric is repaired. Grace is working in every family member, all the time, at any age. When grace wells up, what is important is the person's responsiveness. This eight-year-old and Nick's mother were open at these particular moments. Each of them became an instrument for God's grace to change the other.

Most people experience the reality of sin (tearing the fabric) and reconciliation (mending the fabric) within the family first. One task of the home is to teach how to mend the tears. Ordinary occurrences in the home help us to understand one of the larger church's experiences: a willingness to mend the ruptures of sin, reveling in the joy of God's forgiveness. This is important for the larger church because the fabric of the Body of Christ needs the grace and skill of reconciliation, learned first in the home, in order to stay whole.

Praying

This prayer recalls that we are always in process, always called to engage in the "mending of tears."

1. Take a minute or two to prepare to pray. Use deep breathing, quiet listening, visualization, or whatever works for you to calm your spirit.

2. Bring to mind one relationship that is currently hurting, where some alienation between you and another exists.

3. Try to name the attitude or obstacle in your own self that may be preventing reconciliation. This may or may not be the cause of the alienation. It could be fear, your own inability to take the first step, a past hurt, or a variety of other blockages.

4. Pray the following slowly, thoughtfully, deeply:

> Lord, this block is part of who I am, part of how I feel.
> This is what keeps me separated from _____.
> With your power, change my heart;
> With your power, move me closer to love and forgiveness.
> Amen.

5. Pray the above prayer several times if you want or need to. Make a copy and take it with you as a reminder of God's power to move us to forgive.

If this prayer is to be done in a group, the leader needs to be especially sensitive; this ritual is not meant to be a public confession! The leader should guide everyone through the process, allowing all to reflect within themselves, without speaking aloud. Each participant should make a personal copy of the prayer, "Lord, this is part of who I am . . . ," taking it with them afterward. This should be done in their own handwriting, so each word comes from them individually.

THE STORY TOLD John and Marge

I live next to a longtime married couple. Last night I had dinner with them for the first time since John came back from the hospital about two weeks ago. I could see that John didn't like it one bit, being fed with a large spoon and wearing a dish towel for a bib. It seemed humiliating for him.

Since John's stroke he's lost weight, and he was cranky and critical with his wife, Marge, and with me. Marge coaxed him patiently all the way through dessert. Then she cleaned up the mess, washed his face, and removed the towel from his neck. In their forty-five years of marriage, caring for four children, I could see she had become an expert at cleaning up.

She asked me to help her in what had become their nightly routine. We guided John into the bathroom, holding on to him as he walked shakily. She gave him a bath and dressed him for bed. After they kissed good night, Marge seemed to relax a little, asking me to stay for some coffee. When I said it's marvelous how she's able to take care of John, she acted so casual, like "what else would I do?" She told me that she now sleeps (if you could call it "sleep") in the spare bedroom, waking, listening, noting the slight changes in John's breathing and the familiar cough and throat clearing that comes with his restless nights. And more than likely, she'd have to change his linens during the night too.

Marge spoke freely about the doctor's diagnosis. It could be months before any improvement is noticeable. And there's a very real possibility that John's condition might worsen considerably. That didn't surprise me, but the way Marge said it sure did. She wasn't angry or resentful, just kind of resigned to her role (that doesn't accurately describe her attitude, but I don't know how else to put it).

Marriage is the most remarkable and most courageous of all human acts.

(Ernest Boyer Jr., *Finding God at Home*, p. 17)

Breaking Open the Story

Most of us could understand the difficulty of John and Marge's situation. As couples age, they face the real possibility that this could happen to them.

- ♦ Have you or has someone you know become a caregiver for a loved one?
- ♦ What enables a person to be a caregiver for the long haul?
- ♦ What does the manner of Marge's caretaking say to you?

More Than Meets the Eye

On their wedding day, John and Marge took each other as husband and wife "to have and to hold from this day forward, for better, for worse, for richer, for poorer, in sickness and in health, until death do us part." Like all couples they had no idea where their vows would take them forty-five years later. But their actions now show a deeper appreciation for and understanding of those vows. Their marriage may be seen as a human reflection of the faithful covenant God has made with humanity. The very nature of God is to love, stopping at nothing to care for us, never abandoning us.

The vows John and Marge made proclaimed their intention of "covenant love," which would reveal itself through lifelong acts of faithfulness. Marge's action now witnesses to a lifetime of fidelity.

When couples marry, fidelity may be pledged, but it is usually understood in terms of sexual faithfulness. As the years roll on, faithfulness reveals facets of itself never before imagined: loyalty in conversation, esteem for the other's opinions and feelings, and, as in this instance, respect and care for the life still found in the beloved even though he may be unable to express his mutual love. Covenant love accepts the other exactly as the person is, not the way one partner would like the other to be. John is called to surrender to Marge's care, while Marge is invited to surrender to John's infirmities and inabilities.

John and Marge's love for each other illustrates that marriage and family life are both sign and sacrament, manifesting to the larger world God's ever faithful love for us.

Praying

This ritual prayer is simple indeed! All you need is a small piece of notepaper and something to write with.

1. Write the word *faithfulness* on your piece of paper. Fold it carefully and place it in your pocket, on your calendar, in your purse, or tape it to the bathroom mirror. Each time you see the word or feel the paper, remind yourself of the promises you made to be faithful to your spouse or family. (Such gentle reminders of commitments freely made help us to live them out more attentively.)

2. Right now take a few moments to recall some key people in your life whose faithfulness is a sign for you of God's ever constant love.

3. Give thanks for them; give thanks for your own dedication and faithfulness "for better or for worse, in sickness and in health . . ."

For group prayer be sure to have enough writing materials on hand. If time permits, the group might share who they think of as "signs of faithfulness," and more important, how they are so.

THE STORY TOLD Grandma's Table

Grandma's round oak table occupies a place of honor in our kitchen.

I have all kinds of memories about Grandma's table: standing in the middle of her dining room, covered with big plates of pasta, and surrounded with aunts and uncles and cousins on a Sunday afternoon. There was always animated conversation and lots of stories—some told in Italian so the children wouldn't know what was being said. There were pats on the back for children's accomplishments, serious discussions about the uncles' bakery, and news of relatives living far away.

On the other hand, we had some times of silence and dissension too. I can remember anger and heated disagreements around that table, making a few Sunday dinners hard to digest, and making me feel uncomfortable and unsettled.

The house smelled great for hours before we ate. Grandma cooked long and hard, making most things from scratch. I remember the taste of hot bread from her oven. Every meal began with a "words of gratitude" blessing before the food got passed around by those gathered. There was lots of laughing, arguing, teasing, and enjoying one another—and planning together. And I remember the stories about the past in the old country and about plans for visiting the relatives in California. Even as a little girl at that table, I felt included, as though I was important and my presence was valued too.

Today Grandma's table in my kitchen is still a place of gathering and gratitude. Our meals are rarely made from scratch, but are usually well balanced and the result of someone's taking time and energy to nourish and please the eaters. At the table, family members are encouraged to tell about the day's activities and to share any good news or difficult situations on their mind. There is still arguing, teasing, and enjoying one another's presence. Dinner hours are filled with school practices and jobs, so we gather and gab whenever we can.

The table itself helps to gather people who may initially be strangers into contact with each other, a few feet apart, where gestures, facial expressions, and whispers can be seen and heard. A "family" forms around the table. The revitalization of body takes place through nutrients; the revitalization of spirit, through this community.

(Doris Donnelly, *Spiritual Fitness*, p. 53)

Breaking Open the Story

This heirloom table seems priceless for all the connections this woman makes with previous events, experiences, and the people of her life. The value of Grandma's table lies in associations and ties with the past.

- ♦ What heirlooms hold significant value for you or tie you to the past? What memories do these items evoke?
- ♦ Consider the table on which you and your family eat. Recall some special moments when food and family were inseparable.

More Than Meets the Eye

Tables are built for the eating of meals. But this one, Grandma's table, is also a storehouse of memories. In fact, it has become a symbol within this home, a visible treasure that points to and celebrates so much beyond itself. Its wood has no aura or glow, but this table connects each gathering of today with the countless experiences of previous meals on its surface.

This woman's recollections imply that eating with family and friends is much more than providing food for the physical body. Eating together symbolizes the nourishment of our corporate body— the oneness of family, fostering its common soul. Grandma's table calls to mind patterned actions, familiar smells, and routine family exchanges. Her table serves as the focal point for the domestic church to express what it really is as family: individual members with separate lives melding together as one while eating and gabbing. Laughing, teasing, and exchanging details of the day may seem like ordinary, even routine activities, but these can and do become the means by which God glues individuals together as family. Such gatherings at this table not only express who we are but also make us who we are: one family!

In the hurry-up mentality of today's world, families can easily lose sight of the ordinary yet essential value of gathering communally around the meal table. When done on a regular basis, families can experience a gradual unfolding and sharing of life, both individually and collectively. When nourishing the common body with such attention, the one soul of family has an opportunity to emerge.

What is happening at this family table might be seen as a reflection of what takes place at the eucharistic table of the Lord. The bread and wine shared by Jesus at the table of the Last Supper are the sacred symbols, the "heirlooms" that become for us the risen Lord. Just as the round oak table provides a connection between this family's past and present, the eucharistic table unites past generations (the communion of saints) and present generations of Christians with the risen Lord of all time. At table, the Eucharist both expresses and makes us one body in Christ.

The experience shared around the tables of both the family home and communal worship expresses and, at the same time, makes us, one family in Christ.

Praying

1. Sit at the table where you and your family gather for meals.
2. Pray this blessing prayer adapted from Numbers 6:24–26:

The Lord bless us and keep us;
the Lord make his face to shine upon us, and be gracious to us;
the Lord lift up his countenance upon us, and give us peace.

3. Remember times of gathering around your table; recall the people, the situations—all the details possible.
4. Extend God's blessing to all the family members you've just recalled by again praying reverently the blessing prayer from the Book of Numbers.

5. If at all possible, use this prayer of blessing at your next meal, having everyone repeat each phrase after you.

When offering this prayer as a group, obviously no one will be bringing their dining room or kitchen table to the gathering. So for step 1, ask the participants to visualize their family's common table. After a few moments of quiet, invite everyone to turn to another and describe in full detail their own table. Then continue the ritual as given. Make sure everyone knows the Scripture reference (Numbers 6:24–26) before leaving so that all may pray its blessings with their family.

THE STORY TOLD A Neighborhood Family

Bill and Virginia are an elderly couple who live next door to me to the east, while Lois lives with her mother, Dorothy, one house to the west. Harry and Joan live in the white house at the top of the hill. Harry often refers to himself as "Harry over the hill." Vickie and Mike have two teenage daughters and live one block to the south of my house.

It is not unusual on a cold winter morning after a snowfall to awaken to the sound of Harry scraping his shovel on the pavement in front of my house. He starts at the top of the hill and shovels the snow off the sidewalk all the way past my house to Lois and Dorothy's. I usually leave the house very early in the morning for work. By the time I return home later that evening, Lois has cleared my driveway with her snowblower.

I've often returned home from work to find a message on my answering machine from Harry over the hill, informing me that Joan has some fried chicken or freshly baked goods waiting "just over the hill" for me. Or I arrive home to find a plastic bag filled with tomatoes and cucumbers from Lois's garden sitting inside my front door or hanging from the doorknob.

Recently Virginia had been experiencing some medical problems that required a series of tests and doctor's visits. One day as I pulled into the driveway, I saw that she was outside tending to her beautiful rosebushes lining the driveway. I walked over to where she was working and asked her how she was feeling. She shared with me the ups and downs of the last several weeks, but overall she was hanging in there. She asked me how things were going, and I shared with her that I was going to become a permanent neighbor, as I was in the process of buying the house that I had been living in for the last two years. We chatted a little while longer, and then as we parted, she said, "It will be really nice to have a daughter living next door." I was deeply touched, for I have been away from my own family for ten years and have never been thought of as a daughter by anyone other than my natural parents.

The rest of my neighbors are grateful to Vickie and Mike, who furnish a lawn mower every two weeks or so to contribute to the let's-keep-Carolyn-from-being-kicked-out-of-the-neighborhood campaign, making sure my lawn stays within acceptable bounds as judged by my neighbors. Vickie has been a real angel of mercy, as I have often found much-needed items on my doorstep after a phone call during which I have shared my grocery list and my inability to get to the store. Items such as Kleenex, toilet paper, and six-packs of pop have mysteriously appeared on my front steps without an indication of who has left them or a demand for reimbursement.

> Jesus also extended the prevailing understanding of neighbor. This expansion is so radical that it remains Jesus' deepest challenge to our common-sense way of understanding our relations with other people. . . . "Who is my neighbor?" According to Jesus, a neighbor is anyone in need whom we are able to help.
>
> (William L. Portier, *Tradition and Incarnation*, p. 291)

Breaking Open the Story

This is an exceptional neighborhood! Carolyn presents us with a variety of kindnesses extended among neighbors, from shoveling snow and lending lawn mowers to sharing fried chicken and tomatoes.

- ♦ In what ways does your family go beyond its circle to serve others?
- ♦ In what ways are you served by neighbors or others outside your home?

More Than Meets the Eye

Carolyn's neighborhood is made up of different faces of family. A common trait they share is good neighborliness. All families, by their very nature, are called to serve: these households certainly do! Just as the larger church engages in service and missionary work, so too the home, or domestic church, has a similar missionary spirit. The differences are the arenas and the boundaries wherein the service takes place.

When considering missionary activity, families sometimes look for projects beyond their own borders: donating to food pantries, assisting at soup kitchens, even going to a foreign country. All these are good ways for families to serve others. Carolyn's neighbors are doing their missionary work next door and down the block. Recalling the parable of the good Samaritan, we too might ask Jesus, "And who is my neighbor?" (Luke 10:29). Carolyn and these families take Jesus' parable seriously by serving their neighbors.

The ordinary actions of lending a lawn mower, shoveling snow, sharing vegetables from a garden, and grocery shopping for another are all expressions of Jesus' answer. These neighbors are quietly transforming society into Christ's Kingdom. They're doing it one household at a time, by feeding the hungry, welcoming the stranger, and so on, right on their own street (cf. Matthew 25:40).

Being so helpful, thoughtful, and generous with others takes time to develop. These families (each unique in their own way) began to create a "neighborhood family," one that goes beyond blood relationships. In the process each individual household was enriched, for in serving others, love is multiplied "thirty and sixty and a hundredfold" (Mark 4:8).

Praying

For this prayer you will need some paper and a pen or pencil. Have these at hand as you begin.

1. Write down the names of your own "neighborhood family." As you do so, recall how these individuals have helped you when you were in need: added their joy to your own happiness, said just the right word at the right time, or expressed care for you in some other way.

2. Take a few moments to thank God for this group of people, this neighborhood family, such as they are.

3. Think for a while and identify one way in which you can be an "angel of mercy" to one of your neighbors this week. It doesn't

have to be major or involve vast amounts of your time; sometimes the simplest of gestures can touch another deeply. Circle the name of this neighbor on your list, to remind yourself of your commitment to serve.

For group prayer, writing materials should be provided. After step 1 is completed, invite the group to share some remembrances of care expressed within their neighborhood family. This may become a genuine celebration of goodness received. Follow this with some silent time for internal thanksgiving, leading to the resolution-making of step 3. Again, some group sharing of resolutions may prove beneficial, inspiring one another to deeper levels of care.

Epilogue

The real voyage of discovery consists not in seeking new landscapes, but in having new eyes.

(Marcel Proust)

The real spiritual journey of family consists not in seeking new
landscapes of family living or holiness but in applying depth perception to the circumstances in which we already find ourselves
living. A temptation is to think that a family needs new landscapes
to be holy. Although it is true that sometimes changes need to be
made to better follow God, more often the spiritual journey of a
family is in developing and seeing with depth perception. Through
the family events selected for this book, we have tried to demonstrate the diversity of vistas within family: peaks and valleys; rocky
roads and dead ends; gorgeous, fertile oases and plateaus. These
rich and varied landscapes of family stories have been viewed with
depth perception; glimpses of "God incognito" were recognized—
"God recognito." The one element found at every turn was the
consistent presence of God; all of family life is "crowded with [God]"
(C. S. Lewis), for instance:

- the surprising presence of God while singing "The Housekeeping Blues"
- the expected presence of the Divine at "Benjamin's Baptism"
- the silent, almost tacit presence of generations of God experiences around "Grandma's Table"
- the suffering presence of God in moments of alienation in
  "Wondering Why"
- the letting-go presence of God on "The First Day of Kindergarten"

God is in all and is working through all. As Saint Ambrose says, we but need to see with the "mind and the soul" to recognize the Eternal in the home.

Our God is ever near us, blessing us with richness, being our companion and guide through struggles and suffering. We encourage you to apply depth perception to your present family situations. Pause and remain awake! Then life will go on, opportunities to learn of God will be attended to, revelation will be not only noticed but heeded.

Closing Prayers

We began this book by encouraging you to apply depth perception to your family's lived experiences in order to discover the sacred within. We end by inviting you to continue this process of reflection in the following ways:

1. Obtain a notebook, diary, or journal for your family. It need not be lavish or expensive, just filled with empty pages.

2. Create a cover with the following title: "The _____ Family Sees More Than Meets the Eye."

3. Gather all members of your family for a prayerful dedication of this family book of happenings.

> God, who has loved us into existence,
> we acknowledge your presence in our home, our family,
> and within every individual.
> Bless our home and all who live within.
> We commit ourselves to write the stories and happenings of you,
> active in our lives.
> We want to reflect on these together,
> raising our awareness of your presence.
> We seek to celebrate these as one,
> recognizing your nearness all the more.
> Blessed are you, Lord our God,
> for you are ever present in our life! Amen.

4. Place your family book of stories in an agreed-upon location where all will have access to it. Encourage all family members to record events that clearly reflect God's presence. But don't forget to enter also any events that seem to indicate God's absence. Together may your sharing lead to the discovery of God, present all along.

5. We suggest that you begin a new family tradition. Annually, on the feast of the Holy Family (the Sunday between Christmas and New Year's), read through your family book, noting any patterns, themes, growths, failures, and the like.

After reviewing your stories, consider how you might give thanks to God by celebrating as a family all the ways God has manifested Self in your home.

———◆———

Unwrapping Family Stories

Throughout this book we have modeled a process of seeing with the "mind and the soul" (Saint Ambrose) of the family, looking deeply within the daily exchanges and finding "God incognito" (C. S. Lewis). This process is the skill of depth perception.

Consider the act of unwrapping gifts as a helpful image to clarify this skill. We all love to receive gifts. It's especially exciting, even intriguing, when a present is beautifully wrapped. In fact, the ritual of unwrapping adds a whole new element to the moment.

As adults we realize that the paper, ribbon, tape, and such are not the gift—the gift is within, hidden from sight. Over the years we've grown accustomed to this difference: the skill of pulling tape here, ripping paper there, while being cautious not to break that which might be quite fragile inside.

In much the same way, we as family need to learn how to unwrap our lived experiences. The hidden gift of God's presence, guidance, love, and correction is contained within the wrappings of family arguments, reconciliations, meals, boring chores, celebrations, and whatever else makes up each day of family life. Wendy M. Wright tells us:

> There are times given to us in family life when mystery is glimpsed. Moments of birth and death give us our most heightened experiences. But all moments are potential opportunities to touch the fullness of who we are.
>
> (*Sacred Dwelling*, p. 194)

That potential is realized when we work at unwrapping our family stories.

We want to walk you through the step-by-step process we have used to recognize the hidden gift that is God's presence. It is our hope and prayer that this process (or your adaptation of it) may enable your own "unwrapping" of God's presence in your family. We hope that such a process will assist you in developing depth perception.

Unwrapping the Family Stories

1. **Quiet the mind, body, and spirit.** Relax, close your eyes, take a few deep, cleansing breaths. Become aware of God's presence at this very moment.

2. **Petition God for the eyes of faith.** The five senses alone fail to perceive deeper levels of reality; only faith can move a person beyond mere externals. To experience God's presence and activity, we need to ask for God's assistance in helping us to see our own life as God sees it, for example:

> All-present God, I give you this time for you to use as you see fit. Guide me, surface in me, reveal to me your presence in my family.

3. **Review family events and encounters.**

4. **Focus on one particular happening or relationship** that seems to draw your attention.

5. **Remember the details**: the setting, words, things, and happenings of that moment—the colors, shapes, objects, people, and moods.

Appendix 3 offers a thorough description of a process to develop depth perception. Once you understand and see the rhythm and flow of the entire process, you may find the suggested worksheet in appendix 2 as a short and easy way to walk through this prayerful, reflective process to sense God's "more" in your family life.

Breaking Open the Story

1. Examination of feelings

♦ What feelings come to mind when I recall this particular experience?

♦ If there are negative feelings, take a moment to be present and honest with them.

♦ If there are positive feelings, take a moment simply to savor them.

2. Examination of thoughts

♦ What questions or insights surface as I recall and reflect on this lived experience? Questions and insights may be about the event's meaning or value, about my own identity, or about who I am becoming.

3. Examination of memories

♦ Does my reflection on this one event elicit other related memories?

♦ Notice any patterns or connections (positive or negative) among these memories.

More Than Meets the Eye

1. Dialogue (talk and listen) with God about these feelings, memories, and thoughts.

2. Mindful that we do not come to this dialogue with God empty-handed or empty-minded, recall and ponder any passage from the Scriptures or from spiritual tradition (teachings, poetry, songs, and so on) that offers guidance, comfort, meaning, or hope. (Note: Some experiences are so intense that they may require more time and attention than is appropriate or possible at this point. Turn to appendix 3 for hints in "Matters of Pain and Hurt" or "Matters of Blessing" for further help in this unwrapping process.)

3. Sit patiently with all that has surfaced within you. Ask yourself: How might I trust God's creative hand in the midst of my journey, though I may not know where I'm being led? How might

I give my longing the time it needs to lead eventually to God's fulfillment for me?

4. As you sit with God, do you have a sense or an impression of being called to take some specific action? For example, to reach out, to make a deeper commitment, to grant or to seek forgiveness, to celebrate a blessing, and the like.

Praying

1. Consciously place all that has just happened in God's hands.

2. Create a ritual that expresses the movement of your heart or mind during the preceding process, for example, the use of a gesture or movement, the choice of a family object with related meanings, and so on.

3. Pray for the healing of any family hurts or struggles; give thanks for the blessings of your family.

———◆———

Reflection Process for "Unwrapping Family Stories"

We may ignore, but we can nowhere evade, the presence of God. The world is crowded with Him. He walks everywhere incognito. And the incognito is not always hard to penetrate. The real labour is . . . to come awake. Still more, to remain awake.

(C. S. Lewis, *Letters to Malcolm*, p. 75)

Living artfully, therefore, might require something as simple as *pausing*. Some people are incapable of being arrested by things because they are always on the move. A common symptom of modern life is that there is no time for thought, or even for letting impressions of a day sink in. Yet it is only when the world enters the heart that it can be made into soul. The vessel in which soul-making takes place is an inner container scooped out by reflection and wonder.

(Thomas Moore, *Care of the Soul*, p. 286)

————————◆————————

Quiet the mind, body, spirit . . .
Relax, close your eyes, breathe deeply.
Ask God for the eyes of faith . . .
Try to see your life as God sees it.

1. Recall a family event or situation that is significant for you.
2. Describe the details of the event or situation: the setting, words and actions, persons involved, colors, moods, and so forth.

3. As I recall this situation:

- What feelings—positive or negative—surface in me? Try to remain present to those feelings.
- What thoughts do I have as I recall this situation—about its meaning? about who I am or who I am becoming?
- What memories—pleasant or unpleasant—come to mind?

4. Dialogue (talk and listen) with God about these feelings, thoughts, or memories.

5. Recall and ponder a passage from the Scriptures or from spiritual tradition (teaching, poetry, song, and so on) that offers you guidance, inspiration, comfort, or hope at this time.

6. Offer to God this situation and your present reflection. Pray in thanksgiving or petition; ask for healing or for a special grace. Consciously place all in God's hands.

7. End your reflection time with a ritual gesture or prayer.

APPENDIX 3

———◆———

Growth Toward Wholeness

I am caught up in a story, I mean . . . I can choose to live toward one ending rather than another, toward eternal life rather than death, and I can choose to live out of one beginning rather than another.

(John S. Dunne, *The Peace of the Present*, p. 31)

The power of storytelling is such that a reader gets "caught up" in the story. The family stories told in this book can transport us into a different space within the "soul" of our family. We may come to these stories rather disinterested; however, the evocative nature of the story may move us to laughter, to being tenderly touched, or to tears of sadness and loss. In our experience most of these events elicit an awareness of blessings or of painful, hurtful memories. How each of us chooses to respond to that which is evoked in us is very important, because our response becomes the way we "choose to live toward one ending rather than another."

Every household has a variety of different rooms and places, ranging from the formal living room to the weedy flower patch out back. To manage each of these different spaces requires different talents. For example, the skill to work in the kitchen is different from that used in the den, which is also different from the skill used in the laundry room or on the lawn. In addition, some family members are "experts" in one place, while having little skill in or desire for other spaces within the home. In the same way, we have different rooms and spaces within the "soul" of the family, for example, spaces for joys, sorrows, parties, problems, successes, vacations, tragedies, and routines.

Likewise, to live within these different rooms of the family's soul requires different presumptions and practices. We offer the following presumptions and practices when encountering "matters of pain and hurt" or "matters of blessing" as a means to foster a deeper, more holistic family spirituality.

In Matters of Pain and Hurt

Presumptions

1. **We remember only what we can deal with at any one time in our history.** Do you ever wonder why, "out of the blue," you think of a situation, a happening, a sorrow, a hurt, or a grief that you haven't thought about for a long time?

The body-mind-spirit connection takes good care of us. At times when there is much to do, too many things and people to care for, or when it's not a good time to process, we put some of what we call negative happenings on the back burner.

When something triggers our memory, we re-member, that is, we put it together again. It is at such moments as these that we say to ourselves, "Self, this is an opportunity for reflection, for healing through processing."

2. **God is working through and with us in these moments.** God brings new life out of suffering and death, as manifested in the life of Jesus Christ. Trust that you will discover what you need to know, trust that you will be able to deal with the information you discover, trust that you will be given the grace to move toward healing.

3. **Any sorrow can be borne if we are willing to tell its story.** If you have received the courage to re-member your story, there will be a companion for you on the journey. When we reflect on our happenings, our experiences, we will be given God's amazing grace in the shape of compassion and companionship.

4. **It is not uncommon to get stuck when facing a deep wound.** You may need someone more skilled than a friend to help you sort out the experience.

Practices

1. Sit quietly with a memory, be attentive to it. As the memory unfolds, as it walks across our heart, we might ask ourselves these questions:

- What are my thoughts about myself in this situation?
- In looking back on this situation, as the person I am today, do I have the same perception I had when it happened?
- If I feel hurt, anger, or sadness, how long do I think I need to keep the memory at this intensity of feeling?
- Is there a helpful reason to continue feeling or thinking this way?
- What will be different for me if I let go of this event? What will I lose? What will I gain?

2. Take time to journal about your thoughts and feelings. Journaling is writing without a censor, without analysis, without thought of form. The exercise of journaling may clarify a situation and suggest possible resolutions.

3. Visualize your feelings. For instance, pick up your children's crayons. Look at the various colors; see if a color catches your eye. Begin to use it to express through lines, shapes, intensity of pressure, how and what you are feeling.

4. Create a ritual to fit your situation. Rituals can help you make peace with your past as well as your present fears. Some examples may be a letter written but left unsent, a difficulty symbolically thrown out on trash collection day, a burial ceremony for a particular situation.

5. Consider who would or could be the best listener at this time. Sometimes that which is inside of us cries to be released, to be heard by a listener who will hold us and our story as sacred. Which friend, spiritual guide, or counselor is appropriate for now?

Choose someone who could bring objectivity, respect, wholeness, and knowledge of the faith tradition to your situation. Sharing our stories may be a religious experience in that we allow another to see how God is at work in our own life. And as a listener hears our story, we may learn how God is most truly with us, then and now, in some way.

In Matters of Blessing

Presumptions

1. God is good, generous, and downright extravagant!

The LORD is merciful and gracious,
  slow to anger and abounding in steadfast love.
He will not always accuse,
  nor will he keep his anger forever.
He does not deal with us according to our sins,
  nor repay us according to our iniquities.
For as the heavens are high above the earth,
  so great is his steadfast love toward those who fear him.

(Psalm 103:8–11)

2. Blessings are not simply good luck or the result of good work. **Blessings manifest God's graciousness and overwhelming love.** "And Mary said, . . . 'The Mighty One has done great things for me, and holy is his name'" (Luke 1:46–49).

3. By the power of the Holy Spirit, a variety of gifts are given to the human family. In Galatians, Paul describes a diversity of gifts: "The fruit of the Spirit is love, joy, peace, patience, kindness, generosity, faithfulness, gentleness, and self-control" (5:22–23).

Within families it is not uncommon to discover the Spirit manifested in hospitality, fidelity, perseverance, generativity, trust, extravagant love, delight, innocence, forgiveness, vulnerability, and so forth.

4. Gifts are not given for selfish gain. "To each is given the manifestation of the Spirit for the common good" (1 Corinithians 12:7).

Practices

1. Develop the art of savoring. Savoring is being present to all that is going on and allowing ourselves the time to recognize, enjoy, and appreciate that which is happening in the present moment. Jean-Pierre de Caussade gives us the rationale for savoring: "The present moment is an ever-flowing source of holiness. . . . The present moment always reveals the presence and the power of God" (*Abandonment to Divine Providence*, pp. 49–50).

2. Adopt a posture of thankfulness. Recognize the good that surrounds you, and learn to express it. Gratitude allows us to see the cup of life as half full rather than half empty.

3. Respond as a good and faithful steward. Stewardship envisions all of life as a gift from God. Savoring God's generosity moves us beyond thankful hearts to imitating God: sharing what we have and who we are for the benefit of others.

> From everyone to whom much has been given, much will be required; and from the one to whom much has been entrusted, even more will be demanded.
>
> (Luke 12:48)

Acknowledgments *(continued)*

The scriptural quotations contained herein are from the New Revised Standard Version of the Bible. Copyright © 1989 by the Division of Christian Education of the National Council of Churches of Christ in the United States of America. All rights reserved.

The excerpt by Marcel Proust on pages 7 and 137 is from the Internet, *www.bemorecreative.com/one/206.html.*

The excerpts by Saint Ambrose on pages 8 and 138 are taken from *The Liturgy of the Hours.* English translation by the International Commission on English in the Liturgy (New York: Catholic Book Publishing Company, 1975), pages 491–492. Copyright © 1970, 1973, 1975 by the International Committee on English in the Liturgy (ICEL). All rights reserved.

The excerpts by C. S. Lewis on pages 9, 137, and 140 are from *Letters to Malcolm: Chiefly on Prayer,* by C. S. Lewis (New York: Harcourt Brace and Company, 1992), page 75. Copyright © 1964, 1963 by C. S. Lewis PTE Limited. Copyright renewed 1992, 1991 by Arthur Owen Barfield.

The excerpt on page 10 is from *Twelve and One-Half Keys to the gates of paradise,* by Edward Hays (Easton, KS: Forest of Peace Books, 1981), back cover. Copyright © 1981 by Edward M. Hays.

The excerpt on page 11 is from *The Gaze of Love: Meditations on Art and Spiritual Transformation,* by Sr. Wendy Beckett (San Francisco: HarperSanFrancisco, 1993), page 26. Copyright © 1993 by Sr. Wendy Beckett.

The excerpts by Thomas Moore on pages 12, 56, and 144 are from *Care of the Soul: A Guide for Cultivating Depth and Sacredness in Everyday Life,* by Thomas Moore (New York: HarperCollins Publishers, 1992), pages 286, 258, and 286, respectively. Copyright © 1992 by Thomas Moore.

The excerpts on pages 12, 82, and 122 are from the Vatican Council II document *Familiaris Consortio,* by Pope John Paul II, numbers 17, 36, and 58, respectively.

The excerpt on page 14 is from *To Dance with God: Family Ritual and Community Celebration,* by Gertrud Mueller Nelson (Mahwah, NJ: Paulist Press, 1986), page 33. Copyright © 1986 by Gertrud Mueller Nelson.

The excerpts on pages 17 and 134 are from *Tradition and Incarnation: Foundations of Christian Theology,* by William L. Portier (Mahwah, NJ: Paulist Press, 1994), pages 201–202 and 291. Copyright © 1994 by William L. Portier.

The excerpt on page 20 is from *The Magic Lantern: A Mystical Murder Mystery,* by Edward Hays (Easton, KS: Forest of Peace Books, 1991), page 144. Copyright © 1991 by Edward M. Hays.

The excerpt on page 24 is from *The Rule of St. Benedict in English,* edited by Timothy Fry, OSB (Collegeville, MN: The Liturgical Press, 1982), page 73. Copyright © 1981 by The Order of St. Benedict, Collegeville, Minnesota.

The excerpt on page 26 is from *Webster's New School and Office Dictionary* (New York: World Publishing Company, 1958), page 209. Copyright © 1958 by the World Publishing Company.

The excerpt by Linda H. Hollies on pages 28–29 is from "A Daughter Survives Incest: A Retrospective Analysis," in *Double Stitch,* edited by Patricia Bell-Scott et al. (Boston: Beacon Press, 1991), pages 160–161. Copyright © 1991 by Patricia Bell-Scott, Beverly Guy-Sheftall, and the SAGE Women's Education Press.

The terms quoted on pages 29–30 are from "Turbulence and Tenderness: Mothers, Daughters, and 'Othermothers' in Paule Marshall's *Brown Girl, Brown-stones,*" by Rosalie Riegle Troester, in *Double Stitch,* edited by Patricia Bell-Scott et al., page 163. Copyright © 1991 by Patricia Bell-Scott, Beverly Guy-Sheftall, and the SAGE Women's Education Press.

The excerpt on page 33 is from *By Way of the Heart: Toward a Holistic Christian Spirituality,* by Wilkie Au, SJ (Mahwah, NJ: Paulist Press, 1989), page 50. Copyright © 1989 by Wilkie Au.

The excerpt on pages 34–35 is from the *Dogmatic Constitution on the Domestic Church,* in *Vatican Council II Conciliar and Post Conciliar Documents,* edited by Austin Flannery, OP (Northport, NY: Costello Publishing Company, 1987), number 11. Copyright © 1975, 1986, and 1992 by Reverend Austin Flannery, OP.

The excerpt from the song "We Are Many Parts," by Marty Haugen, on page 36 is taken from *RitualSong: A Hymnal and Service Book for Roman Catholics* (Chicago: GIA Publications, 1996), page 840. Copyright © 1980, 1986 by GIA Publications. Used with permission.

The ancient Aztec Indian prayer on page 37 is taken from *Praying Our Goodbyes,* by Joyce Rupp, OSM (Notre Dame, IN: Ave Maria Press, 1988), page 69. Copyright © 1988 by Ave Maria Press.

The excerpts on pages 44, 68, and 140 are from *Sacred Dwelling: A Spirituality of Family Life,* by Wendy M. Wright (New York: Crossroad, 1989), page 194. Copyright © 1989 by Wendy M. Wright.

The excerpt on page 46 is from *One Minute Wisdom,* by Anthony de Mello, SJ (New York: Image Books, 1988), page 177. Copyright © 1985.

The excerpt on pages 52–53 is adapted from *First Church: A Practical Theology of Family as Domestic Church,* by Joseph A. Torma, PhD (Youngstown, OH: Catholic Diocese of Youngstown, 1992), pages 7–8.

The excerpt on pages 60–61 is from *I Am My Body: A Theology of Embodiment,* by Elisabeth Moltmann-Wendel (New York: Continuum Publishing Company, 1995), page 60. Copyright © 1994 by Gütersloher Verlagshaus, Gütersloh. Translation copyright © 1995 by John Bowden.

The excerpt from "Fruit-Gathering," by Rabindranath Tagore, on page 63 is taken from *On Death and Dying,* by Elisabeth Kübler-Ross, MD (New York: Macmillan Publishing Company, 1969), page 1. Copyright © 1969 by Elisabeth Kübler-Ross.